D0526961

Footprint Handbook
Málaga &
Costa del Sol

ANDY S~~~

C016036930

This is
Málaga

Málaga may be the smallest province in Andalucía, but it compensates with its significant population and economy, much of it based on tourism. The provincial capital is the vastly underrated Málaga, Andalucía's second largest city with a lively nightlife, Picasso museum, trendy shops and some of the region's best tapas bars. The city beach is actually a more attractive strip of sand than many of the gravelly offerings of the Costa del Sol.

The Costa del Sol has a vast influx of Northern European and Spanish tourists every year, and a large expat population. The small-time fishing villages strung along this coast are long gone, swallowed by overdevelopment, a line of beachside hotels and golf courses that stretches almost unbroken the length of the province.

Venture inland, however, and you will discover a more authentic Spain. Towns like Antequera with its prehistoric dolmens have evocative historic appeal, while more recent Moorish influence is seen throughout the region, particularly in architecture and culture. Less than an hour away from the glitzy resort of Marbella, the ancient town of Ronda may be on the coach-tour circuit but is still stunning, set on the El Tajo gorge, while nearby *pueblos blancos* (white villages) are timelessly preserved – and you still need Spanish to order a beer.

Inland mountain ranges include the Serranía de Ronda and the limestone block of El Torcal, with its surrealistic eroded shapes. Rivers have cut deep gorges, such as El Chorro, and many have been dammed to form reservoirs like Guadalhorce. East of Málaga is the dramatic La Axarquía and pretty white villages.

Andy Symington

Best of
Málaga

❶ Cathedral, Málaga city

The city's one-towered cathedral stands proud over the old town. Built in the 16th century, its principal highlight is the stunning choir, whose stalls are backed by beautifully realized sculptures of saints that are some of Pedro de Mena's finest work. Page 10.

❷ Museo Picasso, Málaga city

Occupying a noble palace deep in the heart of historic Málaga's warren of streets, this has a sizeable collection of works by the city's most famous son. It's great to see so many of his works in one place and it gives you a very good overview of his artistic trajectory. Page 11.

❸ The Alcazaba, Málaga city

Perched high over the town, this fortress and the adjoining Gibralfaro castle are sizeable Moorish fortifications which offer stunning views over the city, coastline and the blue sea below. At their base is a Roman theatre. Page 12.

⑤ Málaga's waterfront

The renovated waterfront stretches from the main street of the old town along to the pleasant town beach. It's a picturesque strip made for leisurely strolling, with boat trips, shops and cafés backed by parkland. Page 14.

⑥ La Axarquía

Set back from the coast, this zone of charming hill villages was once notorious bandit country but is now ripe for exploration on foot, with lots of great walks and comfortable rustic places to stay. Page 26.

④ Museo Carmen Thyssen

Though the more famous canvases of Picasso hog the Málaga headlines, this gallery in the pedestrianized centre of the city focuses on 19th-century Andalucían art and does it very well, with romantic depictions of idealized Spanish life. Page 14.

❼ Marbella

The province's most famous coastal resort has plenty of brash tastelessness along the coast nearby, but the town itself is very charming, with a quaint feel to its historic centre and a lively eating scene by the beach. Page 36.

❽ Bobastro

A place of great natural beauty with an appealing solitude, where the ruined fortress of a ninth-century warlord is in a spectacular setting with magnificent views. Page 46.

❾ Antequera

This inland town makes a great stop and has plenty to see. Its enormous prehistoric dolmens are hugely atmospheric, while its impressive collegiate church and fortress tower over the centre. Nearby, a wolf park and impressive natural limestone formations add extra interest. Page 49.

❿ Ronda

The charm of this cloven city comes not just from the gorge that divides it, but also from its wealth of museums and historic buildings, scenic highland surroundings, and status as the cradle of modern bullfighting. Page 52.

Málaga city

Though no more than an airport for millions of sunseekers, Málaga is an important Spanish port and city with plenty to offer, perhaps more than the rest of its province's coast put together. Once bypassed by tourists en route to the beach resorts, these days Andalucía's second largest city is a draw of its own with the Picasso Museum as the main crowd-puller.

Málaga's charm lies in the historic city centre with its narrow pedestrian streets. The long town beach is pretty clean, and there's plenty of good-value accommodation. The city is looking very spruce these days, with the designer boutiques of its central streets overlooked by the Moorish castle. It's also got a great tapas scene and one of Andalucía's liveliest fiestas.

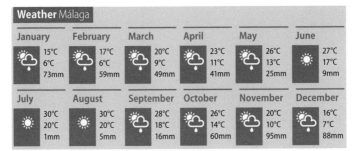

Weather Málaga

January	February	March	April	May	June
15°C	17°C	20°C	23°C	26°C	27°C
6°C	6°C	9°C	11°C	13°C	17°C
73mm	59mm	49mm	41mm	25mm	9mm

July	August	September	October	November	December
30°C	30°C	28°C	26°C	20°C	16°C
20°C	20°C	18°C	14°C	10°C	7°C
1mm	5mm	16mm	60mm	95mm	88mm

Most of the places of interest in Málaga are contained within a compact atmospheric area of 19th-century streets and squares north of the main east–west thoroughfare and can be conveniently visited on foot. Look out for the new Museo de Málaga, whose archaeological and art collections are to be located in the sturdy Palacio de la Aduana near the Roman theatre; it's due to open in early 2016.

★The cathedral and around
C Molina Lario s/n, T952-215917. Mon-Fri 1000-1800, Sat 1000-1700. €5.

Málaga's cathedral, as with many others in Andalucía, was built on the site of a mosque and dates from the 16th century, with numerous modifications at later dates. One of its two towers was never completed, giving it a lopsided appearance, leading to the nickname of *La Manquita*, or the one-armed lady. The interior is both Gothic and Renaissance, while the exterior is typical 18th-century Baroque, aside from a particularly fine Gothic doorway in Plateresque style that dates from the early 16th century.

The highlight of the interior is, without doubt, the **choir**. Behind the stalls are some superb carvings of saints, 42 of which are attributed to Pedro de Mena around 1662 (de Mena's house, now a museum devoted to the painter Revello de Toro, is located in a back street about 500 m from the cathedral). Rearing above the choir stalls are two 18th-century organs. The north entrance, the **Portal of the Chains**, which is usually closed except for Semana Santa processions, is surrounded by a fine screen, carved in mahogany and cedar by Francisco Flores in 1772, with the coats of arms of Felipe II. The admission fee to the cathedral also includes entry to the run-down *museo* near the entrance door, which contains the usual vestments and silver.

There are a number of interesting churches in Málaga centre, the most outstanding being the **Iglesia del Sagrario** ⓘ *Mon-Sat 1000-1200, 1700-1830, Sun 1000-1330*, adjacent to the cathedral with an superb Plateresque *retablo*, and **Nuestra Señora de la Victoria** ⓘ *Mon-Sat 0830-1245, 1800-2030, Sun 0830-1300, €2*, in Calle Victoria, which has further work by de Mena.

Málaga

Málaga has a long history dating back to the Phoenicians, who founded a settlement called *Malaka*, a word derived from *malac*, meaning to salt fish. Málaga became a busy trading port during Roman times, exporting minerals and agricultural produce from the interior. From the eighth century, Málaga was occupied by the Moors, when it was the main port for the province of Granada. It was they, under Yusef I, who built the Gibralfaro fortress in the 14th century. The city fell to the Catholics in 1487 after a long and violent siege.

After the expulsion of the *morisco* population in the mid-16th century, the fortunes of Málaga declined. It was not until the 19th century, when an agricultural-based revival began, that the situation improved. Gradually, the Costa capital began to become a favoured wintering place for wealthy *madrileños*. During the Civil War, Málaga supported the Republicans and the city suffered from the vicious fighting which included an Italian bombardment that destroyed part of its ancient centre.

Over the last 40 years, mass tourism has transformed the neighbouring Costa del Sol, but has thankfully had little damaging effect on the city itself, which remains intrinsically Spanish.

Next to the cathedral on Plaza del Obispo, surrounded by open-air bars and cafés, is the 18th-century **Palacio del Obispo**, or Episcopal Palace, with one of the most beautiful façades in the city.

★Museo Picasso Málaga
C San Agustín 8, T952-602731, www.museopicassomalaga.org. Tue-Thu 1000-2000, Fri-Sat 1000-2100, Sun 1000-2000. Collection €8, exhibitions €4.50, both €10.

This museum has made a significant impact on Málaga; it's put it on the map as a destination in its own right rather than a transport hub for the Costa del Sol. The museum is set in the beautiful Buenavista palace, and the juxtaposition of Renaissance architecture and modern painting has been artfully realized. On display are some 150 Picasso works, mostly donated by his daughter-in-law and grandson. Most phases of the artist's trajectory are represented, from formal portraiture – *Olga con Mantilla* (1917) is a portrait of his first wife – to Blue Period and Cubist works, and many from the later stages of Picasso's life. While the collection will disappoint some, as Picasso's best work is in other museums in Spain and around the world, it's an excellent opportunity to see a lot of his oeuvre in one place. There are regular temporary exhibitions on Picasso or his contemporaries; there is also a café and bookshop here.

Not far away, you can visit the **Casa Natal de Picasso** ⓘ *T952-060215, www. fundacionpicasso.es, 0930-2000, €2*, Picasso's birthplace and now the headquarters of the Picasso Foundation. It is located in the large Plaza de la Merced and has a selection of Picasso's ceramics and lithographs as well as a small selection of his parents' personal objects.

★The Alcazaba

T952-216005, Nov-Mar Mon 0900-1800, Tue-Sun 0830-1930, Apr-Oct Mon 0900-2000, Tue-Sun 0900-2015. €2.25, free Sun from 1400 (€3.55 joint entry price with Castillo Gibralfaro).

Málaga

Where to stay
California **11** *D6*
Casa Babylon **5** *A6*
del Pintor **1** *A4*
Eurostars Astoria **8** *B1*

Molina Lario **4** *B3*
Parador de
  Gibralfaro **12** *B6*
Room Mate Larios **9** *A3*

Restaurants
Antigua Casa
  de Guardia **2** *B2*
Bodegas El Pimpi **25** *A4*
Clandestino **5** *A4*

This former fortress and palace was begun by the Moors in the 700s, but most of the structure dates from the mid-11th century. The site was originally occupied by both the Phoenicians and the Romans and there remains a considerable amount of Roman masonry in the walls. The Alcazaba suffered badly during the Catholic

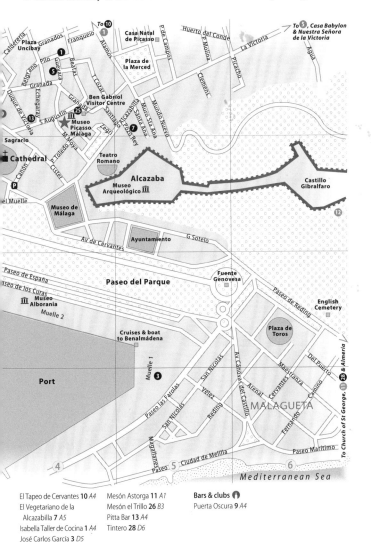

Reconquest, but was restored in the 1930s. Today, it consists of a series of terraced, fortified walls and fine gateways, laid out with gardens and running water in typical Moorish style. There's an archaeological display of pottery and other finds. From the terraces of the main palace building there are fine views over the port and the city.

The Castillo Gibralfaro ⓘ *daily 0900-1800, to 2100 Apr-Oct €2.25 (€3.55 joint-entry price with Alcazaba)*, literally 'Lighthouse Hill', is a ruined Moorish castle built by Yusef I of Granada in the early 14th century. It is linked to the Alcazaba below by parallel walls. A path leads up to it from the right side of the Alcazaba or approach it by the road that leads from the city up towards the parador via Calle Victoria. Alternatively, take the No 35 bus from Paseo del Parque.

Located close to the entrance of the Alcazaba, the **Teatro Romano** ⓘ *C Alcazabilla 8, Tue 1000-1800, Wed-Sat 0900-1900 (2030 summer), Sun 1000-1600, free*, was built in the early first century AD and used for a couple of centuries. Much of the stone was later used by the Moors for their fortresses above, but restoration has left the theatre looking rather spruce. There's a small interpretation centre and information in Spanish and English.

★Museo Carmen Thyssen

C Compañía 10, www.carmenthyssenmalaga.org. Tue-Sun 1000-2000. €6.

The excellent Museo Carmen Thyssen in the centre of town holds a fascinating collection of Andalucian artists ranging from Zurbarán to Julio Romero de Torres. There's also an interestingly wide collection of lesser-known artists whose canvases exhibit traditional regional life. The gallery's focus is on the 19th century. It was a difficult century of invasions and political turbulence in Spain, but you'd have no idea of that from the romanticized depictions of the artists of the time. Gypsies, bullfights, muleteers, priests and dark-eyed beauties ... and they say that Andalucía's cliches were a foreign invention?

The waterfront

renovated port area, a great place for a stroll

★From the Alcazaba, the tree-lined Paseo del Parque is a delightful avenue that runs parallel to the port area and a place of blessed relief on hot summer days.

Muelle 2 runs parallel to Paseo del Parque and includes the small and perhaps overpriced **Museo Alborania** ⓘ *Muelle 2, T951-600108, www.museoalborania.com, Oct-Jun Mon-Fri 1000-1400, 1630-2130, to 2330 weekends, Jul-Sep daily 1100-1400, 1700-midnight, €7*, which has some local fish, touch pools, an opening audiovisual and a very constricted turtle tank. East of here, **Muelle 1** is a new development with shops, boat trips, cycle hire and various eating options.

Further east stretches the city's clean sandy beach, where numerous *chiringuitos* vie for the custom of lovers of seafood and cold beer in the summer months.

A couple of blocks back from the beach, the **English Cemetery** ⓘ *Tue-Sat 1030-1400, Sun 1030-1300, free*, is a beautiful spot that owes its existence to the days when infidels (ie non-Catholics) were buried on the beach, making gruesome reappearances courtesy of storms or hungry dogs. In the mid-18th century, a British consul persuaded the authorities to allow him to start an English cemetery. Look for the small **Church of St George**, a block past the bullring on Paseo de Reding.

From here, a path leads into the leafy walled cemetery, which is a haven of peace. The inscriptions on the gravestones make absorbing reading; there are graves here of many nationalities, the earlier ones covered in shells. The writer Gerald Brenan is buried here alongside his wife, the poet Gamel Woolsey; he had wanted his body to be donated to medical science, but was so well respected by the *malagueños* that none of the members of the anatomy faculty could bring themselves to touch him; he finally arrived here in 2000, some 14 years after his death.

Other museums and galleries

social history and contemporary art

Another of Málaga's Moorish curiosities, Puerta de Atarazañas, is at the entrance to the city market. This was originally the gateway into the Moorish dockyard and it displays the crest of the Nasrid dynasty. The market is vibrant and colourful and well worth checking out.

Anyone interested in social history should see the **Museo de Artes y Costumbres Populares** ⓘ *C Pasillo Santa Isabel 10, www.museoartespopulares.com, Mon-Fri 1000-1700, Sat 1000-1400, €4*, which is located by the dried-up bed of the Río Guadalmedina, a two-minute walk from the Alameda. Look for the inn sign labelled Mesón de Victoria, as this museum is housed in an old 17th-century hostelry. The museum consists of a haphazard collection of everyday items from several centuries ago, including fishing boats, an olive press, guns, farming implements and a range of household relics.

The **Centro de Arte Contemporáneo de Málaga** ⓘ *C Alemania s/n, www. cacmalaga.eu, Tue-Sun 1000-2000, summer 1000-1400 and 1700-2100, free*, is dedicated to contemporary art in all its forms. Outside the entrance, a sculpture of a figure with crumpled shirt and trousers (*Man Moving* by German artist Stephen Balkenholl) sets the tone of *vanguardismo*, which includes contemplative photographic studies and paintings, some of them immense in size and all given optimum display space in 2400 m of white, bright exhibition halls. The aim of the centre is to pioneer new artistic trends through four exhibitions which run concurrently: two temporary shows, another for up-and-coming local artists and a changing, permanent exhibition of pieces selected by renowned modern artists.

The **Museo Interactivo de la Música de Málaga (MIMMA)** ⓘ *Plaza de la Marina s/n, www.musicaenaccion.com, Mon 1000-1400, Tue-Sun 1000-1400 and 1600-2000, €4*, is an atmospheric underground space below Plaza de la Marina, the hub of Málaga. Its collection of musical instruments, variety of recordings, and changing exhibitions among the foundations of the Nasrid city walls focus on both traditional and contemporary musical trends.

Málaga's **Museo del Vino** ⓘ *Plaza de los Viñeros 1, www.museovinomalaga.com, €5, Mon-Fri 1000-1700, Sat 1000-1400*, is located in a restored *palacio* a short walk northwest of the old centre. The modern but slightly functional display takes you through the history and actuality of winemaking in the Málaga area through a series of display panels in Spanish. Guided tours leave according to availability for no extra cost and the guide speaks English. The price of admission includes a tasting of a dry and a sweet wine; you can add extra wines for €1 each.

Concepción Botanical Gardens

a cool escape from the heat of the city and beach

4 km north of the city centre, T951-926180, www.laconcepcion.malaga.eu. Tue-Sun 0930-2030, until 1730 in winter, last entry 1 hr before. €5, guided tour, with multilingual guides, for 1½ hrs. Easy access, well signposted off the Málaga–Antequera autovía, just off the Ronda de Málaga; get bus No 2 and walk 10 mins north; city sightseeing tour buses also head out there Tue-Sun from the bus station.

These botanical gardens are well worth a visit and have an interesting history, being created over 150 years ago by Amalia Heredia and her husband, the American George Loring, a mining tycoon, who later became the Marquis of Casa-Loring. They collected plants from many parts of the world and also accumulated an important archaeological collection. The visit leads to a mirador giving stunning views over Málaga (the cathedral and castle are clearly visible) and the enormous stone dam of La Concepción reservoir.

Listings Málaga city *map p12*

Tourist information

Regional tourist office
Pasaje Chinitas 4, T952-213445, otmalaga@andalucia.org. Mon-Fri 0900-1930, Sat and Sun 0930-1500.

Municipal tourist office
Pl de la Marina, T952-926020, www.malagaturismo.com. Daily 0900-1800 (2000 Apr-Oct).
Between the port and the centre, this tourist office has free city audio guides, plus various self-guided walking tours. At C Granada 70, near the Picasso museum, is the Ben Gabirol visitor centre. There are also smaller tourist offices at the airport and bus station, plus several information kiosks in the centre.

Where to stay

There's a good range of accommodation for all budgets in the central area around the Alameda near the port. Prices go up in summer; some cheaper options at this time include university residences, which you can reserve via www.booking.com.

€€€€ Parador de Gibralfaro
Paseo García del Olmo, T952-221902, www.parador.es.
In a dreamy setting, surrounded by pine trees, next to the Moorish castle with

panoramic views. The rooms are simply yet tastefully decorated with warm colours, woven rugs and terracotta tiles. There are private entrances and sun terraces. The restaurant dishes up regional and international fare. Have a drink on the terrace even if you're not staying here and take in the vista. Booking essential.

€€€ Hotel Molina Lario
C Molina Lario 20, T952-062002, www. hotelmolinalario.com.
Near the cathedral, this 4-star choice successfully spreads itself to appeal to both the work traveller, with sleek design and business facilities, and families, with kid-friendly staff, and a rooftop pool and terrace to relax. The rooms are spacious, sparklingly clean and stylishly modern; those facing the street are the most appealing. Recommended.

€€€ Room Mate Larios
Marqués de Larios 2, T952-222200, www. room-mate hotels.com.
This has an upbeat feel to match its top location on Málaga's swanky pedestrian shopping street. The cheerful yet elegant decor features black and white tiles, cream, maroon and warm-toned furnishings and plenty of light wood. Try for a room overlooking the bustling Plaza de la Constitución, although it can be noisy on a Sat night. You can get some very good deals on the website, depending on the date.

€€ Eurostars Astoria
C Comandante Benítez 5, T951-014300, www.eurostars hotels.com.
Slick 3-star hotel near the Contemporary Art Gallery and Alameda train station, for trains to the airport. Rooms are spacious with plenty of gleaming marble and light wood. Excellent value for the price with

many extras including hydromassage in the en suite bathrooms and internet access in all rooms. You can get cheaper deals on hotel booking websites.

€€ Hotel California
Paseo de Sancha 17, T952-215164, www. hotelcalifornianet.com.
Near the beach at the eastern end of town, this is a friendly hotel with unremarkable but spacious rooms despite the ominous name. The staff are very helpful and it represents significant value for this coastline.

€€ Hotel del Pintor
C Alamos 27, T952-060980, www. hoteldelpintor.com.
Handily located just on the edge of the old quarter, in easy striking distance of Picasso attractions, this bright white modern place features small but attractive rooms – grab an interior one to avoid the street noise – and friendly staff.

€ Casa Babylon
C Pedro de Quejana 3, T952-267228, www.casababylonhostel.com.
Laid-back but facility packed, this backpackers in a suburban house offers comfortable new bunks, an instant Málaga social life, cheap beer and free internet. The only downside is it's a bit of a trek from the centre of the action. Breakfast included.

Restaurants

There are some very convivial restaurants where you can enjoy traditional local specialities, such as *fritura malagueña* (fried fish), washed down with Málaga's famous wine, a sherry-like substance that comes in sweet and dry varieties. Many of the best fish restaurants as well as *chiringuitos* on the sea can be found in the suburbs of Pedregalejo and El Palo.

€€€€ José Carlos García
Muelle 1, T952-003588, www. restaurantejcg.com.

In a luminous minimalist dining room on Málaga's new waterfront promenade, this takes traditional Andalucían ingredients and gives them a stunning gastro-molecular twist. The degustation menu is €110 plus drinks and, on a good day, it's worth every penny.

€€ Bodegas El Pimpi
C Granada 62, T952-228990, www. elpimpi.com.

Near the Picasso Museum, this labyrinthine former wine warehouse offers atmosphere in spades, with local sweet and dry drops in barrels signed by famous folk who've been here. If you can grab a table (it's big but often packed), you can snack on traditional Andalucían dishes, but the ambience is better than the food. There's a pleasant terrace around the back opposite the Roman theatre.

€€ Clandestino
C Niño de Guevara 3, T952-219390, www. clandestinomalaga.com. Daily 1300-0100.

This inventive and intensely popular brasserie can resemble a student canteen at first sight, with its chunky wooden tables, relaxed bohemian ambience and scurrying staff. Don't be fooled, as the cuisine is classy and inventive; they aim high, and if they don't always reach, they still comfortably clear most of the places around here.

€€ El Tapeo de Cervantes
C Cárcer 8, T952 609 458, www. eltapeodecervantes.com.

Intimate and charming, one of Málaga's best tapas options is a couple of blocks north of Plaza de la Merced. You might have to wait for one of the few tables, but it's worth it, with excellent traditional dishes backed up by some highly original creations.

€€ Isabella Taller de Cocina
C José Denis Belgrano 25, T951-130018, www.isabellatallerdecocina.com.

This sweet little place can be hard to find but it's worth it. Grab a seat outside if you can – or take a high table by the bar – and enjoy really excellent, innovative and generously proportioned dishes. It's an unusual menu, with North African and other Mediterranean influences, and the originality and quality are outstanding. Recommended.

€€ Mesón Astorga
C Gerona 11, T952-342563, www. mesonastorga.com.

It's worth the walk out to this welcoming place near the train station for an excellent Málaga dining experience. Top-quality produce, including great grilled meats and fresh fish, is backed up by interesting wines and a genuinely Spanish atmosphere. Recommended.

€€ Mesón el Trillo
C Don Juan Diaz 4, T952-603920, www. grupotrillo.es.

This warm and convivial spot is an atmospheric tapas stop. Excellent wines are available by the glass, and there's a big range of bar food, from *trillos* served on toasted bread, to *revueltos* and delicious chopped steaks. There's also a restaurant menu, served in the spacious interior or on the terrace, but not quite as much love goes into the food, it seems.

€€ Tintero
Playa del Dedo, El Palo, T952-206826, www.restauranteeltintero.com.

One of the most entertaining restaurants (with another branch near Cártama). Waiters bear dishes non-stop into the dining area, shouting what they've got on offer. If you fancy it, grab it from them; nearly all dishes have a standard price. Fried fish is the main thing to try here. It's fast, entertaining and extremely noisy.

€ Antigua Casa de Guardia
Alameda 18, on the corner of C Pastora, T952-214680, www. antiguacasadeguardia.net.
Founded in 1840, this wonderfully atmospheric bar seems to have changed little since then. It opens at 1000 in the morning and starts filling old men's glasses with delicious Málaga wines from the row of barrels behind the bar. A little seafood stall dishes out prawns and mussels as the perfect accompaniment to a chilled *seco*. A photograph on the wall shows a youthful Picasso knocking one back here. Recommended.

€ El Vegetariano de la Alcazabilla
C Pozo del Rey 5, T952-214858.
One of several vegetarian restaurants around town, this has a handy location at the foot of the Alcazaba and a pleasant quiet terrace. Home-made wholemeal pasta, plenty of salads, vegan dishes and a very tasty mushroom *pil-pil*. On weekdays there's a generous mixed plate for not many euros.

€ Pitta Bar
C Echegaray 8, T952-608675.
Tucked around the corner from the Picasso Museum, you'll find Middle Eastern tapas like falafel, hummus, *baba ghanoush* and tabbouleh. Great for vegetarians. There's a terrace on the street too.

Bars and clubs

The main central nightlife zone is just north of C Granada in the streets around C Luís de Velázquez. Plaza Merced also has some options, while on Plaza Marqués del Vado del Maestre, just off C Calderería in the centre, there are also several bars, whose customers merge outside on the square. There is a host of disco-bars south of the bullring, in the Malagueta area, whereas nightlife in the summer months tends to spill out towards El Palo and its beachside discos.

Puerta Oscura
C Molina Lario 5, T952-221900, www. puertaoscuramalaga.com.
One of the classiest in Málaga, this 19th-century bar-café has chandeliers, alcoves and classical music. It's the best – though certainly not the cheapest – place for that late-night coffee and liquor. Recommended.

Festivals

Easter Semana Santa, when religious brotherhoods organize daily processions with huge and elaborate floats carrying sacred *paso* figures through the streets of the city. It's one of Spain's best Easter celebrations.
23 Jun San Juan, sees huge bonfires on the beach, live concerts and all-night partying.
16 Jul Virgen del Carmen's effigy is taken by a procession of boats out to sea by fishermen.
Aug Feria, with bullfights, flamenco, processions and fireworks. There are 2 venues: during the day festivities take place in the streets surrounding C Marqués de Larios; in the evening it moves to the fairgrounds on the outskirts

of the city where one of Spain's biggest parties kicks off night after night. All the *casetas* are open to the public, and most serve food as well as drinks.

Shopping

The main shopping area is west of the cathedral and north of the Alameda Principal and in streets around the Plaza de la Constitución. The Larios shopping centre, between El Corte Inglés and the bus station, has over 100 shops, a hypermarket and a multi-cinema.

What to do

Bike tours and hire
Bike2Malaga, *C Vendeja 6, T650-677063, www.bike2malaga.com*. Near the Plaza Merced, these people offer bike hire for €5/10 for a half/full day and also give guided city tours.
Málaga Bike Tours, *Pasaje La Trini 6, T606-978513, www.malagabiketours.eu*. These people take you on good-natured 2-wheeled tours of town for €24, includes a drink in a bar. They also rent bikes for €5/10 for a half/full day.

Boat trips
Cruceros Pelegrín, *Muelle 1, T687-474921, www.barcosdemalaga.es*. Run hour-long cruises from Muelle 1, costing €10, with regular departures throughout the day.

Football
Málaga, now owned by a Qatari investor, have a lot of support, partly from the expat crowd. Games are held at the **Estadio de Fútbol La Rosaleda**, Av de Martiricos, T952-614374, www.malagacf.es.

Golf
There are over 40 golf courses along the Costa del Sol to the west of the city. The nearest, and the oldest course on the coast, is **Real Club de Campo de Málaga**, T952-376677, www.rccm-golf.com, 4 km east of Torremolinos. It's state owned and attached to the Parador de Golf hotel.

Transport

Air
Málaga's international airport, T952-048844, www.aena-aeropuertos.es or the good unofficial page www.malagaairport.eu, is located 7 km west of the centre. A taxi will cost you €15-20. The cheapest transport to centre is the Fuengirola–Málaga train, every 30 mins from 0700 to midnight (€1.70 single). The journey takes 15 mins. There are 2 Málaga stations; the final Centro-Alameda stop is more central. There are also buses (€3) 0700-midnight from the airport (from the Alameda to the airport at 30-min intervals between 0630 and 2330).

Málaga has a busy airport which handles 12 million passengers a year. **Air Europa**, **Vueling** and **Iberia** and its subsidiaries run internal flights to several Spanish cities. Numerous budget airlines from all over Europe fly to Málaga, some only in the summer. See Getting there, page 99, for more details.

Bus
The bus station is conveniently close to the main train station on Paseo de los Tilos, southwest of the centre. It's a 20-min walk to the centre or take a local bus.

A complete timetable is available from the tourist office. There are hourly buses from the bus station (T952-350061, www.estabus.emtsam.es) to **Granada** (2 hrs). Buses to **Sevilla** leave a few times daily (2 hrs 45 mins). Buses to **Córdoba** leave 4 times daily (3 hrs), and there are many buses along the coast in both directions.

Car hire

All the main international firms have offices at the airport. Local Spanish firms are also represented. As ever, the best deals are to be found online via broker websites. Smaller firms have their offices on the airport approach road, to which they will transport customers by minibus (allow 30 mins for this when departing). A reader-recommended operator here is **Helle Hollis**, Av del Comandante García Morato, T952-245544, www.hellehollis. com. Offices in the city include: **Avis**, C Cortina del Muelle, T952-216627, www. avis.com; and **Hertz**, Alameda de Colón 17, T952-225597, www.hertz.com.

Ferry

There are regular daily sailings (except Sun mid-Sep to mid-Jun) to **Melilla**, the Spanish enclave in North Africa. The crossing takes around 8 hrs.

For further information contact **Trasmediterránea**, C Juan Díaz 4, T902-454645, www.trasmediterranea.es.

Taxi

There are taxi ranks at the bus and train stations and on Alameda Principal. **Radio Taxi**, T952-327950. One of several companies.

Train

The main train station is near the bus station on Paseo de los Tilos, a 20-min walk to the centre, or hop on a bus.

There are 11 daily **AVE** trains to **Madrid** (2 hrs 30 mins, €80), which travel via **Córdoba**, also served by cheaper trains (1 hr). Except on Sun, there's a daily morning train to **Ronda** (2 hrs), stopping at **Alora** and **El Chorro**. There are 6 daily slow trains and 6 daily fast trains to **Sevilla** (1¾-2½ hrs) as well as services to other Andalucían cities.

The **Fuengirola**–Málaga *cercanía* line is planned eventually to extend to **Marbella** and Estepona in the west, and Nerja in the east and has another branch running north to **Alora**. Purchase tickets from the machines on the platform.

East from
Málaga

Traditionally more Spanish in character, the eastern Costa del Sol is facing a rapidly increasing influx of tourists and retirees from northern Europe and is changing its nature quickly.

Nevertheless, Nerja is attractive, having not yet been spoiled by the ribbon development that has ruined much of the western part of the province.

Nerja

spectacular location on a low cliff, backed by impressive mountains

Despite rapid recent growth, Nerja, some 50 km east of its provincial capital, still retains considerable charm in its narrow, winding streets and dramatic setting. There are sandy coves, long beaches and, despite a spiralling increase in residential tourism, most of the new buildings and *urbanizaciones* have been aesthetically designed. Nerja's caves east of town pull the crowds and make a dazzling venue for the annual summer festival. Nerja also has excellent places to stay and eat.

Sights

Today, the local economy is largely reliant on tourism. There is also a large foreign community who have made Nerja their permanent home. Architectural controls here mean that there are few high-rise hotels and the centre is still old fashioned with narrow winding streets flanked by bars, souvenir and speciality shops.

At the heart of the town is the famous **Balcón de Europa**, a balmy, palm-lined promenade with magnificent views over the rocky coastline. To the west of here is the whitewashed **Church of El Salvador**, dwarfed by its Norfolk pine. It has elements of *mudéjar* and baroque work, plus an interesting mural representing the Annunciation on a Nerja beach.

There are still a few fishing boats on the **Playa Calahonda**, just east of the Balcón, but the most popular beach, just out of sight behind the headland, is **Burriana**, which is packed during the summer and offers a whole range of watersports, ranging from waterskiing to kitesurfing. Small cove beaches in town are easily accessed via stairs, and have dark, pebbly sand and quite sharp drop-offs in the water.

BACKGROUND

Nerja

Nerja started life as the Moorish settlement of *Narixa*, but an earthquake in 1884 destroyed much of the town and no Moorish constructions survived. For centuries the inhabitants eked out a living by making silk, growing sugar cane and fishing. None of these activities thrive today and the sugar refining buildings are part of the industrial archaeology. Nerja is famous in Spain for having been the setting for the iconic early 1980s TV series *Verano Azul*.

Cuevas de Nerja

Ctra de Maro s/n, T952-529520, www.cuevadenerja.es. Winter 1000-1300, then guided visits 1300 and 1600-1730, summer 1000-1830, guided 1100-1200, 1830-1930. €9, 6- to 12-year-olds €5. The caves are just above the N340, and clearly signposted from it. Parking costs €1. There are regular buses from Nerja, or it's a 30-min walk or 10-min drive.

These limestone caves 5 km from Nerja were discovered in 1959 by a group of local schoolboys on a bat-hunting expedition and are now a major tourist destination, with busloads rolling up every day of the year. The most important finds were the wall paintings, probably Upper Palaeolithic in age and largely of animals, believed to be part of a magical rite to ensure success in hunting and guarantee the fertility of domestic animals. Regrettably, the paintings are not on public view. The guided visit takes just under an hour; the lighting of the caves and the piped music may appear to some visitors to be somewhat overdone, but the limestone features are genuinely awe-inspiring. The caves are far more extensive than you get to appreciate on the tour, but you can get to grips with further sections by booking a day's caving (October to June, booking via T680-207135 or the website, over-14s only). The day includes drinks, sandwiches, equipment, guide and around five to six hours of exploration. In the summer season, the main chamber of the caves is used as an auditorium for a festival of music.

Listings Nerja

Tourist information

Tourist office
C Carmen 1, T952-521531, www.nerja.es. Mon-Sat 1000-1400, 1700-2045, Sun 1000-1345.
Just across from Balcón de Europa, the tourist office occupies the ground floor of the town hall.

Where to stay

There is a good choice of accommodation to suit all pockets. It is best to book in advance during summer and Semana Santa.

€€€€ Parador de Nerja
C Almuñécar 8, T952-520050, www. parador.es.
The only disappointment here is that, unlike many paradores, the building is not

a historic palace or even that old. On the plus side, the location is perfect: on a cliff edge with rooms overlooking the garden and sea and a lift that drops you right down on the beach. Some rooms have whirlpool baths and private patios. The restaurant is recommended, particularly the seafood; try the giant *langostinos*. There's also a pool and tennis court.

€€€ Balcón de Europa
Paseo Balcón de Europa 1, T952-520800, www.hotelbalcon europa.com.
With an unbeatable location right on the Balcón itself, this has bright and spacious rooms, decorated with elegant simplicity. The hotel is built in the rock face so the entrance is on the 6th floor (from the Balcón), while rooms have direct access to the private beach below. A good place to relax, with a piano bar, sauna and massage. Rooms with views and balcony cost more, but are memorable.

€€€ Hotel Carabeo
C Carabeo 34, T952-525444, www. hotelcarabeo.com.
A delightful English-owned boutique hotel down a quiet side street near the centre. The furniture and decor throughout is sumptuous with tasteful antiques and paintings by acclaimed local artist, David Broadhead. There's a range of rooms (some are €€), including sea-view suites with great views and a private terrace. The elegant restaurant serves delicious modern Mediterranean cuisine and tapas. Recommended.

€€-€ Pensión Miguel
C Almirante Ferrándiz 31, T952-521523, www.pensionmiguel.net.
A very appealing option on a pedestrian street near the Balcón de Europa, this renovated Andalucían townhouse offers good-value accommodation in bright and cheerful rooms with fridge and private bathroom. The owners are exceptionally helpful; there's also a lovely roof terrace with views – perfect for tasty breakfast or romantic sunset. Minimum 2-night stay in high summer. Recommended.

€ Hostal Tres Soles
C Carabeo 40, T952-525157, www. hostal3soles.com.
This small, central and helpful option is behind a greenery-covered façade on a pedestrianized central street with easy access to beaches. Rooms are simple and comfortable, offering decent value. A little more gets you an apartment with kitchenette and balcony. Upstairs rooms offer a better outlook. Breakfast available.

€ Mena
C El Barrio 15, T952-520541, www. hostalmena.es.
A good location in the narrow backstreets west of the Balcón. The rooms in this friendly 10-room *hostal* are spotless, bright and cheery with interesting artwork. There's a pretty patio, and the best rooms have a balcony overlooking the cliff-top garden for only €5 more.

Camping

Nerja Camping
T952-529714, www.nerjacamping.com. Closed in Oct.
Located around 5 km east of town on the N-340, the campsite is leafy and spacious, but the place gets busy in summer so book ahead. It's significantly cheaper off season.

Restaurants

There's a wide selection of restaurants to suit all pockets and tastes. Seafood restaurants are moderately priced here. Many restaurants close for part or all of the winter. Beware of inflated prices in the bars and restaurants around the Balcón.

€€€ Oliva
C Pintada 7, T952-522 988, www. restauranteoliva.com.
Stylish and popular, this is a reliable choice for upmarket but unpretentious dining. Plenty of thoughtful touches are allied with well-presented modern cuisine.

€€ El Pulguilla
C Almirante Ferrándiz 26, T952-523872.
Typical of Málaga province with its no-nonsense stainless steel and tiles, this bar pulls in the crowds for its good-quality fried fish and other seafood snacks. There's also ice-cold Cruzcampo beer, generous wine pours, and a free tapa with every drink.

€€ La Marina
Plaza de la Marina, T952-521299.
Famous locally for its fish and seafood, cooked *a la plancha* (grilled), *hervido* (boiled), or *a la sal* (baked in salt). Simple yet uses the freshest ingredients.

€€ Lan Sang
C Málaga 12, T952-528053, www. lansang.com.
This spot is an excellent and authentic Laotian and Thai restaurant with top-notch service, and attractive wooden tables. The food (all coded by spiciness and content) ranges from cracking fish curries to tasty vegetable stir-fries. Try the *khao niew* sticky rice, meant to be eaten balled up in your fingers.

€ Esquina Paulina
C Almirante Ferrándiz 45, T952-522181.
An intimate, well-run and charming place, this offers quality wines, tasty gourmet tapas, fine *tablas* of ham or cheese, as well as coffee, cakes, and cocktails.

Bars and clubs

Disco and karaoke bars cluster around Plaza Tutti Frutti (yes, that is its real name), just west of the main road, running down to the water. By night in summer, the **Papagayo** beachside restaurant turns up the volume with live music (from flamenco to hard rock) and DJs until sun-up.

Entertainment

Flamenco
El Molino, *C San José 4, www.facebook. com/elmolinonerja.* Nightly show at 2100 and a good, not-too-touristy atmosphere.

Festivals

Feb Carnaval for 3 days with parades and singing of *chirigotas* (popular songs).
16 Jul Fiesta de la Virgen del Carmen, the fishermen's fiesta; the statue of the Virgin del Carmen is carried down to the sea at Calahonda beach.
9-13 Oct Feria de Nerja, local saint's day and a week-long festival.

Transport

Bus
There are buses more than hourly to **Málaga** (1 hr) and the coastal towns to the west; and several daily buses eastward to **Almuñécar**, **Granada** and **Almería**. Local buses head to and from the inland villages of the Axarquía, such as **Frigiliana**, **Torrox** and the hospital at **Vélez Málaga**.

Car
It's relatively easy to park on the edges of town or at the underground car park in the centre (follow signs for Balcón de Europa). It's pricey but very handy.

La Axarquía

★This popular walkers' region was once notorious bandit country and later a guerrilla stronghold during and after the Civil War. Like the Alpujarra in Granada province, it preserves a distinctly North African character: the remains of the Moors' labours in creating terracing and irrigation channels can still be seen, while the small villages dotting the area are whitewashed, with narrow streets.

The main settlement of the region, Vélez Málaga, isn't a particularly enticing place, as it is rapidly succumbing to overdevelopment fuelled by expat demand. The same is gradually happening to most of the villages – the only buildings not for sale are the estate agencies – but the region still has ample charms and offers some rewarding walking. It's better to pick up tourist information on the region before arriving; contact the offices in Nerja and Málaga.

In an effort to encourage rural tourism, five routes have been devised for visiting La Axarquía by car, each colour coded and waymarked. Owing to the terrain, most of the routes are not circular and involve retracing one's steps in places, but they are, nevertheless, recommended. A detailed brochure describing the routes can be obtained from the tourist office in Nerja. Be prepared, in the more remote parts of La Axarquía, for some erratic signposting.

The Ruta del Sol y del Aguacate (the Sun and Avocado Route) starts at Rincón de la Victoria and visits the agricultural villages of the Vélez valley, including Macharaviaya, Benamacarra and Iznate. The Ruta del Sol y del Vino (the Sun and Wine Route) starts in Nerja and includes the main wine-producing villages, such as Cómpeta and Frigiliana. The Ruta Mudéjar concentrates on architecture, looking at villages, such as Archez, Salares and Sedilla. The Ruta de la Pasa (the Route of the Raisin) looks at the more mountainous villages in the northwest of the area. Finally, the Ruta del Aceite y los Montes (the Route of the Oil and the Mountains) examines the olive-growing villages, such as Periana and Alaucín in the north of the area.

Vélez Málaga

The so-called capital of the Axarquía is only 4 km from the coast and is more of a gateway really, as it has little in common with the villages of the area apart from being steeply located on a hilltop. It wasn't reconquered by the Christians until 1487, and still preserves some of its Moorish fortress on a crag above the town. The parish church of **Santa María la Mayor** was built on the site of the main mosque, whose minaret has been converted into the belltower. There's a fine *mudéjar* ceiling inside.

Vélez Málaga has no tourist office, though there is one on the coast in Torre del Mar, so the offices in the villages of Sayalonga, Cómpeta and Frigiliana are the best places for information on the Axarquía region.

Cómpeta and around

Despite the large numbers of northern European expats, this village is still one of the best spots to relax in the Axarquía. The hills around are stocked with Moscatel grapes that are used to make a sweet wine. The main square is overlooked by the **Iglesia de la Asunción**. Nearby, on the main road, is a small **tourist office** ⓘ *T952-553685, turismo@competa.es, Apr-Oct Mon-Sat 1000-1500, Sun 1000-1400, winter closed Mon-Tue*; this is also where the bus stops. You can obtain local walking maps at the office.

Sayalonga and Archez

From the coast at Caleta de Vélez, a road snakes up into the hills towards Cómpeta via the typically picturesque villages of Sayalonga and Archez. The former has a **tourist office** ⓘ *T952-535206, oficinadeturismo@sayalonga.es, Mon-Fri 1000-1500*. It's in the square at the end of the only road through this narrow village. Leave your car on the main road to explore the village, as you'd probably have to back it out again.

The village's main attraction is the **Cementerio Redondo**, which is indeed round. Sayalonga is also the start of a pleasant walk (see the Sayalonga circuit, below).

Not far beyond, and signposted left off the main road, **Archez** is another sleepy, pleasant place with a good place to stay and eat.

Frigiliana

Frigiliana, a mere 6 km from the coast and steeped in Muslim atmosphere, was the site of one of the last battles between the Christians and the Moors in 1569 and ceramic plaques record the events on the walls of the houses in the older part of the town. With narrow streets and whitewashed houses festooned with hanging plants and geraniums, it's perhaps the region's prettiest village, although also its most touristy. For the best view of the surrounding valley with its Mediterranean backdrop, climb up to the mirador with its handy bar and restaurant. The **tourist office** ⓘ *Plaza del Ingenio, T952-534261, www.turismofrigiliana.es, mid-Sep to Jun Mon-Fri 1000-1730, Sat-Sun 1000-1400, 1600-2000, Jul to mid-Sep Mon-Fri 1000-1530, 1700-2100, Sat-Sun 1000-1400, 1600-2000*, can provide information on accommodation.

Alfarnate

In the northwest of La Axarquía, not far from Antequera, is Alfarnate. On the road outside the village, the **Antigua Venta de Alfarnate** ⓘ *T952 759388, www.ventadealfarnate.es, 1000-1800*, is claimed to be the oldest inn in Andalucía. Once the haunt of assorted highwaymen and robbers, including the notorious El Tempranillo, it now houses a small outlaws' museum including a prison cell. The characterful *venta* serves country food and is cheerfully crowded with Spanish families at weekends.

Walking in La Axarquía

magnificent Mediterranean and mountain views

What makes walking in La Axarquía such a treat is the very marked difference in climate, vegetation and terrain between the higher passes and the coastal fringe. The Mediterranean is often visible, sparkling in the distance, and on most of the walks the Sierra de Tejeda provides a spectacular backdrop, especially during the winter months when there is often snow on its higher reaches. Many walks in the area are waymarked.

The best maps of the area are the standard 1:50,000 map of the Servicio Geográfico del Ejército, Series L. The walks mentioned below are covered by maps: Zafarraya 18-43 and Vélez-Málaga 18-44. The Marco Polo bookstore in Cómpeta generally has both maps in stock.

Sayalonga circuit → *Distance: 10 km. Time: 3½-4 hrs. Difficulty: easy.*
This half-day excursion links two attractive villages, Sayalonga and sleepy Corombela. The walk takes you through the subtropical orchards of Sayalonga's terraced river valley where there is an astonishing variety of fruit trees. Then comes a steep climb up to Corombela passing by several small farmsteads and on the return leg there are excellent views of the Sierra de Tejeda and the Mediterranean.

Nearly all the walk is along tracks and this is an easy circuit to follow. There is a short section of tarmac road when you leave Corombela but there is very little traffic; don't let this put you off this walk. **Map**: 1:50,000 Vélez-Málaga (1054).

Canillas de Albaida circuit → *Distance: 11 km. Time: 4½-5 hrs. Difficulty: medium.*

This enchanting walk takes you out from Canillas de Albaida via a beautiful riverside path, which meanders through thick stands of oleander, crossing back and forth across the Cájula river – easily passable unless there has been heavy rainfall. After a steep climb the middle section of the walk takes you along dirt tracks and is quite different in feel. But it is easy to follow and there are fine views of the Sierra de Tejeda. The final section of the walk – there is a steep climb last thing – is along an ancient cobbled path with gorgeous views of Canillas and the Chapel of Santa Ana. Try to do this walk when the oleander is in flower for a real spectacle. There are some prickly plants on the middle section before you reach the forestry track so you could wear trousers. **Map**: 1:50,000 Zafarraya (1040).

Itinerary The walk begins from the car park at the entrance of Canillas as you come from Cómpeta. Go down the hill from the roundabout past the supermarket and chemist. At the bottom bear left at a sign for 'Finca El Cerrillo'. Head down past the chapel of San Antón then bear right and drop down, cross the river then immediately bear right following a concrete road towards an old mill. The road narrows to a path that runs beside the Cájula river, crossing back and forth several times. Pass a breeze-block building (20 minutes) on your left and continue along the river's right bank. You'll see red waymarking. Cross the river again and climb; there is beautiful old cobbling in places. After passing beneath an overhanging rock face you descend back down to the river, cross it a couple more times, then the path climbs up the river's left bank between two fences and becomes a track. Ahead you will see a white farmhouse.

Be careful! Before you reach it, branch right (by a small orange tree to the left of the track) at a sign 'Camino del Río' along a narrow path that passes by a grove of avocados. It winds, passes the stumps of a line of poplars, then continues on its rather serpentine course, occasionally marked by cairns. Shortly your path is crossed by another, which has black water pipes following its course. Turn right here and then almost immediately left, then wind down to the river that you cross via stepping stones. The path climbs up the other bank and soon becomes better defined (occasional red dots mark the way). Where the path divides go left. A ruined house comes into sight on the other side of the river. Cross the river again and climb the path towards the house. You should pass just to the right of the house then climb steeply up the side of the valley. As you climb you'll see a solitary building on the crown of a hill. Remember this landmark – you'll pass by it later in the walk. The path swings right, descends, crosses a (dry) stream, then bears right again and winds uphill. You come to an area of terracing where you continue to climb. Above you to your right you'll see a small farmhouse. Head up to the farm that you should pass just to its right. You reach a dirt track. Turn right here (one hour, 15 minutes) and head for the solitary building which you saw earlier in the walk. Just past the house the track arcs left towards the head of the Cájula gorge and a small cluster of houses. The track winds, descends, crosses el Arroyo de Luchina via a concrete bridge with rusting railings, then climbs again past olive and citrus groves. After passing a house to your right, where a row of pines has been planted, you cross the river (one hour, 45 minutes). Continue past a row of poplars on the main track: don't turn sharp right on a track leading down towards the river. Follow this track, climbing at first, roughly parallel to the Río Cájula, heading back towards Canillas. Eventually you pass a water tank then a house to the right of the track with a solar panel (two hours). Just past this house the track swings to the left and another track branches right (it has a chain across it). Ignore this turning, continue for 30 m and then – careful! – turn right away from the track on to a beautiful path that zigzags all the way down to the river Llanada de Turvilla. Somewhere to one side of the path would make a memorable picnic spot. Cross the bridge over the river then bear right and wind up towards the Santa Ana chapel. Pass beneath the chapel – the gorge is now down to your right – and after a steep climb the path becomes a track that leads you just beneath the cemetery where a green mesh fence runs to your right. Bear sharp left past house No 35, go to the end of the street then head up the hill past the supermarket and bank to arrive back at your point of departure.

Listings La Axarquía

Where to stay

There are many *casas rurales* in the Axarquía region. Check with local tourist offices or visit www.toprural. com for a good selection.

Cómpeta and around

€€ Hotel Alberdini
Pago la Lomilla 85, T952-516294, www. alberdini.com. If coming from Sayalonga, turn right towards Torrox just before entering Cómpeta.
Perched on a hill with wonderful views over the surrounding valleys, this rustic stone-clad rural hotel makes a relaxing base. Rooms are decorated in individual styles, and there's a restaurant, other good facilities and various activities like Pilates and Spanish classes. There are various free-standing bungalows,

including one rather curious cave-like one. Prices are very reasonable.

€ La Vista Cómpeta
C Panaderos 43, T625-857318, www. lavistacompeta.com.
This charming whitewashed place nestled high in the village offers sweet simple rooms and gorgeous roof terraces plus a small plunge pool. Rates are a bargain and include breakfast, served alfresco.

Apartments

There are numerous houses for holiday rentals available in the village; ask at the tourist office or in one of the estate agents.

Sayalonga and Archez

The tourist office in Sayalonga plus online brokers have details of a number of village houses for rent, either for a night or for a longer stay. Prices vary.

Frigiliana

€€€-€€ Hotel Los Caracoles
Ctra Frigiliana-Torrox Km 4.6, around 5 km west of Frigiliana, T616-779339, www.hotelloscaracoles.com.
One of the more unusually designed hotels in southern Spain, this has 5 striking bungalows (*caracoles*, or snails), that are romantic shell-shaped structures blending *modernista* architecture with North Africa via Greece and *Star Wars*. They are equipped with salon, bedroom and bathroom and have a double room and a sofa bed. There are also enchanting doubles with terrace, and a restaurant that has some Mozarabic-style dishes and cracking views over coast, hills, and villages.

€€ La Posada Morisca
Ctra Frigiliana–Torrox Km 2, T952-534151, www.laposada morisca.com.
A couple of kilometres west of Frigiliana, this is an enchanting spot, and utterly relaxing. All rooms have views of the coast from their balconies, and elegant rustic-style decor. They also have wood-burning stoves and decent bathrooms. There's a good restaurant (dinner only) and a small pool.

Restaurants

See also the hotel listings for good eating options.

Cómpeta and around

€€ Museo del Vino
Av Constitución s/n, T952-553314, www. museodelvinocompeta.com.
This isn't a museum but a shop. It deals out generous glasses of local wine, which you can accompany with traditional tapas of ham, chorizo or cheese. There's also a restaurant serving classy roast meats. It's a little tacky, but the food and service is good.

€€ Restaurante El Pilón
C Laberinto s/n, T952-553512, www. restaurantelpilon.com.
On a steep street below C San Antonio, this Brit-run restaurant has an upstairs terrace and dining rooms with great views over the village and the hills beyond. It's warm and busy. Book ahead in summer.

Festivals

Cómpeta and around

15 Aug The boisterous **Noche del Vino** festival where you can enjoy the local wine.

Frigiliana

20 Jan Fiesta San Sebastián when villagers walk barefoot through the streets carrying candles and the statue of San Sebastián.
Aug Annual **dance and music festival**, with plenty of *fino* and fiesta spirit.

Transport

Vélez Málaga

There are several daily buses from **Málaga** and frequent connections from **Torre del Mar** and **Nerja** on the coast.

Cómpeta and around

There are 3 daily buses to Cómpeta from **Málaga** via **Vélez Málaga**.

Frigiliana

Regular buses run from Torrox to Frigiliana.

Costa del Sol

The Costa del Sol is a curious mix of paradise and hell, a stretch of ribbon-developed coast where sun-blessed retirees rub shoulders with corrupt mayors and mafiosos looking for the next dodgy property deal.

To impoverished Franco-era Spain the influx of tourists was a blessing; now, with competition from other holiday destinations in the Mediterranean and Caribbean, the concrete jungles can seem more of a curse, and the lack of foresight in approval of developments, not to mention the bribes taken to rubber-stamp them, is staggering.

Nevertheless, despite the timeshares and the crimes against architecture, it remains a good-time zone. Spain's former property boom meant that facilities improved, and it's not just a spot for cheap beer and a lobster tan. The ever-increasing numbers of 'residential tourists', generally middle-aged northern Europeans looking to live out their retirement years with a bit of decent sunshine has boosted the local economy and meant that the seaside towns aren't so reliant on the whims of the sun-seeking package tourist.

While not even the Costa del Sol's biggest fan could describe the beaches as anything more than gritty, nor the cultural attractions anything more than token, the climate remains exceptional, and the ambience cheery. Still, it can seem like the least Spanish of places, with northern European languages dominant. In July and August resorts are very crowded.

Once a byword for all the worst aspects of Mediterranean tourism, Torremolinos has long been surpassed in crassness by other destinations and, if visited off season, can actually be quite pleasant.

It is difficult to appreciate that 50 years ago there were hardly any buildings here apart from the water mills that gave Torremolinos its name (and which stopped working in 1924), and a few fishermen's cottages behind La Carihuela beach. The centre of what old town existed is Calle San Miguel, now a busy pedestrianized alley full of boutiques, restaurants and a Moorish tower. Torremolinos has four beaches; for the best sand, atmosphere and restaurants head for La Carihuela, the old fishermen's quarter, with the most appealing part of the maritime promenade. There are three **tourist offices** ① *one at Bajondillo beach, Plaza de las Comunidades Autónomas s/n, T952-371909, one in La Carihuela, C Delfines 1, T952-372956, and one in the centre on Plaza Independencia, T952-374231.*

Torremolinos merges imperceptibly into Benalmádena to the west. The name applies to both the pretty *pueblo*, 300 m above sea level, and the beachside development. The beach is one of the Costa's best, and there's an attractive marina where various companies offer boat trips out into the Mediterranean. There are also a couple of family-friendly attractions. Within the marina is **Sea Life** ① *T952-560150, www.visitsealife.com, daily 1000-1800, to 2000 May-Jun and Sep-Oct, to midnight Jul-Aug, €15.50, children €12.50,* a submarine park with plastic tunnels taking you into the aquarium for eyeball-to-eyeball contact with sharks, jellyfish (no eyeballs) and other sea creatures. It's substantially cheaper to book via their website. While travelling along the N340 you'll see the **Teleférico de Benalmádena** ① *T952-577773, www.telefericobenalmadena.com, return trips 1100 until dusk plus night trips Jul-Aug, closed Jan to mid-Feb, €7.40/€13.25 single/return,* a cable car swinging above the road to the top of the Calamorro mountain, 769 m above sea level. The journey takes 15 minutes and there are fantastic views; you can even spot Morocco on a clear day. Hikers can enjoy a choice of several trails when they reach the top. Alternatively, there's a bar, donkey rides and regular bird-of-prey displays.

Listings Torremolinos and Benalmádena

Where to stay

Torremolinos
There are plenty of rooms except at the height of the season. Most large package tour hotels are behind the eastern beaches; you get better rates for these booking through agencies. The best place to be based is La Carihuela.

€€€€ Hotel Amaragua
C Los Nidos 3, T952-384700, www. amaragua.com. 4-day minimum stay in season.
In La Carihuela near Benalmádena marina, this is a sizeable and striking seafront hotel, with plenty of space, decent rooms, all with balcony, most

with sea views (although these can be noisy). The location is good, and it feels more Spanish than British. There's a pool and spa, and standard 4-star facilities.

€€ Hotel Cabello
C Chiriva 28, T952-384505, www. hotelcabello.com.
This small family-run hotel is a block back from La Carihuela beach. Rooms are clean and simply furnished; most have a sea view. There is a small bar with an adjacent small lounge with a pool table. Good value, especially outside of Aug, when it's €.

Bus
Regular buses run along the coast road between **Málaga** and **Fuengirola** (45 mins) via Torremolinos. There are also many services on to **Marbella** and a number of long-distance services from Fuengirola to other Andalucían cities as well as **Madrid**.

Train
Torremolinos is a stop on the **Fuengirola–Málaga** railway, trains run every 30 mins in each direction.

Fuengirola and Mijas

lively resort and more Spanish than most of this coast

Fuengirola

A mere 20-minute drive from Málaga airport, Fuengirola is both a popular holiday spot and a genuine Spanish working town, with a busy fish dock and light industry in the suburbs to the north. It appeals to northern European retirees in the winter, when it feels fairly staid, and attracts large numbers of Spaniards in the summer, when it doesn't.

The main **tourist office** ⓘ *Av Jesús Rein 6, T952-467457, www.visitafuengirola.com, Mon-Fri 0930-1400, 1630-1900 (2000 in summer), Sat 1000-1300*, at the old railway station, can provide maps and information.

Unlike Torremolinos, Fuengirola has a long history. Extensive Roman remains have been excavated; it was they who probably built the first structure at the **Castillo de Sohail** located on a hill by the river at the west end of the town. The castle was destroyed in 1485 in the Christian reconquest of the area, the Moors surrendering on the day of San Cayetano, the patron saint of Fuengirola today. In 1730, the castle was rebuilt to defend the coast against the British who had taken Gibraltar in 1704. During the Peninsular War in 1810, a British expedition of 800 men under General Blayney landed at the castle and advanced on Mijas, but later they retreated to the castle, where, humiliatingly they were obliged to surrender to 150 Polish mercenaries. At this time the population of Fuengirola was a mere 60 people; today, it is closer to 50,000. The Castillo de Sohail interior is now an outdoor auditorium where concerts take place. There is also a small exhibition centre/museum.

The small zoo **Bioparc Fuengirola** ⓘ *Av José Cela 6, T952-666301, www. bioparcfuengirola.es, daily 1000 until dusk, to midnight in Jul-Aug, €17.90, children €12.50*, is an excellent example of humane treatment. There are no cages and four different habitats create a natural environment for the animals. The zoo is also heavily involved in conservation programmes and focuses particularly on African and Asian rainforest species. A majestic baobab tree is another highlight.

Mijas

Mijas is geared to the tourist (foreign residents outnumber Spaniards by two to one in the Mijas administrative district), with donkey rides, garish souvenirs and English-run restaurants. Despite all this, Mijas has a certain charm and is worth a visit. It has a long history, going back to Roman times, while the Moors built the defensive walls that partially remain today. The village is located 425 m above sea level at the foot of steep mountains. The *vista panorámica* in well-kept gardens above the cliffs gives superb views along the coast. There's a **tourist office** ⓘ *Plaza Virgen de la Peña s/n, T952-589034, www.mijas.es, Mon-Fri 0900-1800 (2000 summer), Sat 1000-1400.*

Housed in the former town hall, the **Mijas Museum** ⓘ *Plaza de la Libertad s/n, daily summer 1000-1500, 1700-2200, winter 0900-1900, €1*, has various themed rooms, such as an old-fashioned bodega and bakery, and regular exhibitions are held in the gallery upstairs.

Donkey 'taxis' are popular in Mijas, and are now being looked after better thanks to the monitoring of a donkey sanctuary. Standard rates are €10-15 for a ride, or €15-20 to be pulled in a donkey cart.

Listings Fuengirola and Mijas

Where to stay

Fuengirola
Many hotels have reduced rates in winter.

€€ Las Islas
C Canela 12, T952 375 598, www.lasislas.info. Easter-Oct.
Unpromisingly set in the narrow lanes of the Torreblanca district, this romantic hotel is quite a surprise with its relaxing tropical vegetation, sizeable pool and colourful, comfortable rooms with views. The on-site restaurant does some Lebanese dishes among other fare. Recommended.

Camping
There are numerous sites close to the sea to the west of Fuengirola.

Mijas
The Mijas area has plenty of hotels.

€€ El Escudo de Mijas
C Trocha de los Pescadores 7, T952-591100, www.el-escudo.com.
Spotless, attractive rooms in a friendly location in the heart of Mijas *pueblo*.

Restaurants

Fuengirola
There is a vast and cosmopolitan range of choice in Fuengirola; however, the standard often leaves much to be desired. Head to C Capitán for a few more traditional eateries. Tapas bars are located mainly in the area to the west of the train station and on C San Rafael, which leads off the main square.

€€ Bodega El Tostón
C San Pancracio, T952-475632, www.bodegaeltoston.com.
A good tapas choice, decked out like a traditional Madrileña bodega with a vast selection of wine, served in enormous goblet-style glasses and accompanied

by complimentary canapés or more filling fare.

€€ Mesón Salamanca
C Capitán 1, T952-473888, www. mesonsalamanca.es.
A reliable option for good solid Castilian cuisine just off the main square on a street with several decent choices. It's traditional in feel and generous in portion.

Mijas
If you head for the Plaza de la Constitución, there are several restaurants with stunning views down to the coast.

Festivals

Fuengirola
16 Jul Fiesta de la Virgen del Carmen.
The statue of the Virgin is carried from the church in Los Boliches in a 2-hr procession to the beach and into the sea. An amazing spectacle, with half the inhabitants on the beach and the other half either swimming or in boats.
1st 2 weeks of Oct Feria del Rosario takes place on the showground site between Los Boliches and Fuengirola, where there are *casetas* for the various societies and brotherhoods. All this is accompanied by fireworks, bullfights and flamenco.

Transport

Bus
Most of the bus services are run by **Portillo**, T902-450550, www.portillo. avanzabus.com.

Marbella
the most interesting of the Costa del Sol towns

★In Spain, the name Marbella conjures up a host of images. As the place where many of the country's celebrities spend summer, it has glamorous connotations; Spain's tabloid press relocates here in August to keep track of A-listers hanging out in the latest glitzy nightclub. But Spaniards always knew there was plenty of sleaze behind the diamanté façade – Jesús Gil y Gil, an infinitely corrupt man, was mayor here for years; after his death, the police investigation Operación Malaya opened a stinking can of worms, centred around cash-for-development approval scandals and money-laundering.

Nevertheless, Marbella is still by far the best place to stay along this coast, if you stay in its picturesque old city or on the beach below. Here, there are excellent places to stay and eat, and a lively atmosphere all year. West of the centre, however, a hideous strip of pleasure palaces, plastic surgery clinics, and Ferrari repair shops line the road to Puerto Banús, a luxury marina and hubristic exercise in the poorest of taste. Cracking summer nightlife yes – but it's a depressing triumph of style over substance and reeks of Eastern European mafias and local corruption.

Sights
Marbella's **Casco Antiguo** (Old Town) is a compact area located to the north of Avenida Ramón y Cajal. In its centre is the pretty **Plaza de Naranjos**, opened up in the 16th century by the Christian town planners who demolished the maze of

Marbella has a long history, having been populated at various times by Phoenicians, Visigoths and Romans, as well as being the most important Moorish town between Málaga and Gibraltar. Historians suggest that Moorish Marbella was a fortified town, with an oval shaped, 2-m-thick encircling wall containing 16 towers and three gates – to Ronda, Málaga and the sea. The town was taken by the Christians in 1485 and they set about remodelling the layout of the fortress, but much of the Moorish street plan remains today.

The changes began in the mid-1950s when a Spanish nobleman named Ricardo Soriano introduced his friends to the area. His nephew, Prince Alfonso von Hohenlohe, built the **Marbella Club**, attracting a wealthy international set to the area. Marbella's inhabitants include Arab royalty, stars of the media, famous sportspeople and members of Russian mafias. A visitor to Marbella might be surprised at its reputation as life seems entirely normal on the surface, but the glitzy social life is there going on behind closed doors in luxury yachts, palatial villas and private clubs.

Former mayor Jesús Gil actively promoted Marbella as a sort of Spanish Montecarlo, but ran up huge debts, and was staggeringly corrupt. He had friends in high places but, once he died in 2004, his lackeys and co-conspirators found themselves in an exposed position. The police investigation Operación Malaya saw some three billion euros in cash and valuables – paid for by illegally appropriated public funds – seized, and over a hundred notables sent to prison at some point, including the late Gil's protégé, Julián Muñoz, and Muñoz's lover, the famous copla singer and darling of the celebrity pages, Isabel Pantoja.

alleyways that comprised the Moorish *médina*. On the north side of the square is the 16th-century **Ayuntamiento** (town hall). In the southwest corner of the square is a delightful stone fountain, the **Fuente de la Plaza**, which dates from 1604. Nearby is the **Ermita de Nuestro Señor Santiago**, Marbella's oldest church, a small and simple building thought to date from the late 15th century. Look also for the **Casa Consistorial**, built in 1572. It has a fine wrought-iron balcony and *mudéjar* entrance, while on its exterior stonework is a coat of arms and inscriptions commemorating the bringing of water to the town. Finally in the square is the **Casa del Corregidor**, with a 16th-century stone façade, now a café.

Head for the northeast corner, particularly around Calle Trinidad, where there are good stretches of the old Moorish walls and at the western end of this street stands one of the towers of the original *Castillo*, built by the Moors in the ninth century. The old walls continue into Calle Carmen and Calle Salinas. Also at the east end of the old town in Calle Misericordia, is **Hospital Real de San Juan de Dios**, which was founded by the Reyes Católicos at the time of the Reconquest to minister to foreign patients. It has a chapel with a panelled *mudéjar* ceiling and a tiny cloister.

The **Museo del Grabado Español Contemporáneo** ① *C Hospital Bazán s/n, T952-765741, www.mgec.es, Mon and Sat 1000-1400, Tue-Fri 1000-1430, 1700-2030 (1800-2200 summer), €3, under 18s free*, an exhibition of contemporary Spanish prints, is housed in the sympathetically restored **Palacio de Bazán**. This Renaissance building with an attractive exterior of pink stone and brickwork was originally bequeathed by its owner Don Alonso de Bazán to be a local hospital.

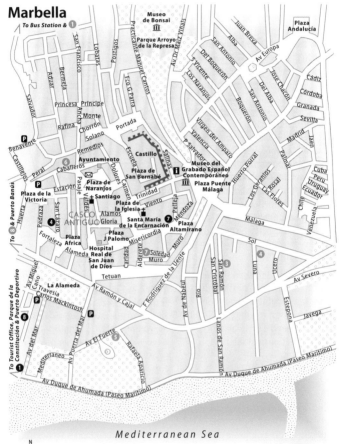

Marbella

Mediterranean Sea

100 metres
100 yards

Where to stay 🛏
Albergue Juvenil **1**
Central **3**
El Fuerte **5**
Hostal Enriqueta **6**

La Luna **4**
Marbella Club **8**
Town House **7**

Restaurants 🍴
Bar Altamirano **7**
El Estrecho **4**
La Venencia **8**
Santiago **1**

In the Parque Arroyo de la Represa, a series of terraced gardens and lakes to the east of town, the **Museo de Bonsai** ⓘ *Parque Arroyo de la Represa, T952-862926, daily 1030-1330, 1600-1830 (1700-2000 in Jul/Aug), €4*, is housed in a modern building surrounded by landscaped gardens and lakes. The miniature trees are imaginatively displayed on a wooden raft-like structure over water containing turtles and fish in Japanese style.

The **Museo Ralli** ⓘ *CN-340, Km 176, T952-857923, www.rallimuseums.com, Tue-Sat 1000-1500, closed mid-Dec to mid-Jan, free*, located in the Coral Beach complex a few kilometres to the west of Marbella, isn't dedicated to wrestling cars through forests, but is rather a light and airy collection of fine Latin American art and sculptures, as well as some paintings and graphic designs by Picasso, Dalí, Miró and Chagall. It's a very worthwhile visit.

Listings Marbella *map p38*

Tourist information

Tourist office
Glorieta de la Fontanilla s/n, T952-771442, www.marbellaexclusive.com. Mon-Fri 0900-2100, Sat 1000-1400.
On the main promenade, the tourist office is helpful. There's another *turismo* (C Salinas 4, T952-761197, Mon-Fri 0930-2000, Sat 1000-1400) in the old town, with town maps.

Where to stay

Most of Marbella's hotels are on the outskirts. There's good budget accommodation within the old town itself.

€€€€ Hotel El Fuerte
Av El Fuerte, T952-861500, www.fuertehotels.com.
One of the few hotels in the centre, this is a charming older building dating back to the 1950s and renovated recently. Most rooms have balconies with sea views (substantially more expensive) and the furnishings are traditional with plenty of dark wood. There is a lovely palm-filled garden with a pool situated between the hotel and the beach, just a few paces away. Recommended.

€€€€ Marbella Club Hotel
Bulevar Príncipe Alfonso von Hohenlohe s/n, T952-822211, www.marbellaclub.com.
The **Marbella Club** opened its doors almost 60 years ago and has since become part of the Marbella tradition. The level of luxury is exemplary and facilities include a golf resort and riding stables, thalassotherapy spa and exclusive hair salon. The rooms, however, don't always live up to the hype, and you might be better off in one of the villas, which have their own garden area. There's also a smart restaurant, pool, gym, and a host of other 4-star facilities. You may get better rates from a travel agent. Think €450+ for a double in summer.

€€€ The Town House
C Alderete 7, T952-901791, www.townhouse.nu.
An appealing boutique B&B in a great location in the old town. It's very elegant, with white walls and furnishings offset by works of art. The rooms vary

substantially; some are cosy, some more spacious. Best of all is the relaxing roof terrace – a quiet drink after a day at the beach goes down a treat here. Breakfast is included. Recommended.

€€ Hostal Enriqueta
C Los Caballeros 18, T952-827552, www. hostalenriqueta.com.
Close to Plaza los Naranjos, this has spacious, clean, good-value rooms with bathroom and friendly management. It's particularly well priced off season. You can put the car in the underground public car park right by the *hostal*. Recommended.

€€ Hotel Central
C San Ramón 15, T952-902442, www. hotelcentralmarbella.com.
This has a superb location on a pretty flower-flanked pedestrian street in the old town. The rooms are cheery, with chessboard tiles, and small balconies; go for one overlooking the patio garden. All have a/c and free Wi-Fi access; there's also a cosy sitting room with fireplace furnished with antiques. Prices are very reasonable.

€€ La Luna
C La Luna 7, T952-825778, hostallaluna. wordpress.com.
The rooms here are situated around a central terrace. There are fans and fridges and the rooms are a good size and squeaky clean – so much so that owner Salvador will refund your money if you find so much as a speck of dust! Peaceful and friendly. There are several other good budget options in these narrow pedestrian streets east of the centre if it's full.

€ Albergue Juvenil
C Trapiche 2, T951-270301, www. inturjoven.com.

Andalucía's best official youth hostel is just above the old town, and is a great, spacious facility with the bonus of a pool (summer only). Rooms vary in size, but are clean and modern; there's also disabled access, and a more-than-decent kitchen.

Camping
There are a few excellent campsites near Marbella, all on the coast road, close to the beach. All are open year round. Booking is advisable Jul and Aug and during fiesta time.

Restaurants

There is a glittering array of eateries in Marbella, including several of Andalucía's best.

€€€ La Meridiana
Camino de la Cruz, Las Lomas, T952-776190, www.lameridiana.es.
Just west of town near the mosque with upbeat Moroccan-style decor and an enclosed patio for year-round alfresco dining. The menu includes roasts and fish dishes like *lubina grillé al tomillo fresco* (grilled sea bass with fresh thyme). Quality is trumped by high prices here, but the atmosphere can make it worth it for a romantic evening.

€€€ Santiago
Paseo Marítimo 5, T952-770078, www. restaurante santiago.com. Closed Nov.
Appropriately located just across from the beach, this is a Marbella fish classic. The seafood here is catch-of-the-day-fresh with lobster salad a speciality. This is a popular restaurant with well-heeled locals, who wisely ask the professional staff for the day's recommendation. Meat dishes are also available, and the place also runs 2 tapas

bars, 1 specializing in stews, around the corner. Recommended.

€€ Bar Altamirano
Plaza Altamirano 4, T952-824932, www. baraltamirano.es.
This buzzing place is vastly popular with locals and tourists around, so get there early to bag your table and enjoy the well-priced *raciones* of rather tasty seafood and fish bought fresh from the market that morning. It's no-nonsense and traditional in feel and all the better for it. A real highlight is the warm and professional service.

€€ La Venencia
Av Miguel Cano 15, T952-857913, www. bodegaslavenencia.com.
In this promising tapas zone between the old town and the beach, this is the most outstanding choice. There's an excellent range of cold and hot plates; you can't really go wrong. There's cheerful seating around barrels both inside and out, and top service. Recommended.

€ El Estrecho
C San Lázaro 4, T952-770004, www. barelestrecho.es.
This reliable old tapas haunt is a well-established favourite on a narrow street off Plaza de la Victoria. It's full of locals enjoying the cheap and tasty morsels dished over the bar; the *albóndigas* and *ensaladilla rusa* stand out from the herd. Look out for the curious frieze depicting the social life of dogs. The Bartolo, opposite, specializes in fried fish and is also worthwhile.

Bars and clubs

Most of the action in the area takes place in Puerto Banús, rather than Marbella. From Marbella, buses run regularly from Av Ramón y Cajal just below the old town. In Marbella itself, most of the evening action is around Plaza Los Olivos at the top of C Peral in the old town, or in the port area, where there are a couple of dozen bars in a row – take your pick.

Festivals

Easter Semana Santa processions.
Jun Feria y Fiesta de San Bernabé celebrates Marbella's patron saint with concerts and firework displays.

Shopping

Good-quality shops abound in Marbella, particularly along Av Ricardo Soriano and in the alleyways of the old town. Many specialize in expensive jewellery and fashion goods. There are also numerous art galleries and craft shops.

What to do

Golf
Marbella is surrounded by golf courses, including **Río Real**, T952-765732, www. rioreal.com; **Aloha**, T952-907085, www. clubdegolfaloha.com; **Los Naranjos**, T952-812428, www.losnaranjos.com; **Las Brisas**, T952-813021, www.realclub degolflasbrisas.es; **Guadalmina**, T952-883375, www.guadalminagolf.com (at San Pedro) and **La Quinta**, T952-762390, www.laquintagolf.com (road to Benahavís).

Transport

Air
The nearest airports are Málaga and Gibraltar, both accessible by road in under an hour. The nearest train stations are Algeciras to the west and Fuengirola to the east.

Bus

Most of these bus services are run by **Portillo**, T902-450550, www.portillo. avanzabus.com.

There are regular buses to and from **Málaga**, some express (50 mins), and some go via **Fuengirola** (45 mins) and **Torremolinos**. There is also a Málaga airport bus that leaves from Marbella bus station 10 times daily between 0530 and 2200. Heading west, there are regular buses to **Algeciras**, some via **Estepona**.

Other cities served include **Sevilla**, **Madrid**, **Granada**, **Ronda**, and **Cádiz**. The main bus station is in C Trapiche, next to the bypass, but most local buses pass through the town centre.

Around Marbella

laid-back resort, attractive whitewashed settlements and views of North Africa

Ojén

Just 8 km north of Marbella is the expanding village of Ojén, which has a history going back to Roman times. A number of springs rise in the village and this attracted the Moors who were in power here until 1570 and Ojén still retains much of the flavour of that time. It was once famous for the production of *aguardiente*, a powerful *anís*, but its main claim to fame today is the annual **Fiesta de Flamenco** during the first week in August. Ojén also has an interesting parish church that was built on the site of a mosque.

Continue through Ojén and over the pass and after 4 km turn left through the pine forests to the Refugio de Juanar and a walking track that leads through woodland of sweet chestnut, almonds and olives to a mirador at 1000 m, from where there are stupendous views over Marbella, the coast and, on clear days, Morocco. Allow 1½ hours for this walk. The wildlife is incredible, with a wide range of flowers, including orchids, butterflies and birds. Small family groups of ibex are not uncommon; during the spring and autumn, migratory birds of prey can be seen en route to and from the Straits of Gibraltar, while booted and Bonelli's eagles breed in the vicinity. The area can be crowded with picnickers on Sundays.

Estepona

Perhaps the most low-key and relaxed of the Costa del Sol resort towns, likeable and family-friendly Estepona has a long seafront backing a clean shingle beach. It's a quiet place, more a home for the grey diaspora than young funseekers, but has a few picturesque corners. It has an enthusiastic **tourist office** ⓘ *back from the beach at Av San Lorenzo 1, T952-802002, turismo@estepona.es, winter Mon-Fri 0900-1500, Sat 1000-1330, summer Mon-Fri 0900-1930, Sat 1000-1330.*

Outside of town north of the motorway, **Selwo Aventura** ⓘ *Autovía Costa del Sol Km 162.5, T902 190 482, www.selwo.es, €24.50 for over-9s, open 1000-dusk mid-Feb to Oct plus weekends in Nov-Dec,* is a popular safari park where you can see various 'respect' animals from a truck that takes you around the complex. There are also various activities on offer. You can save almost 50% by booking a week in advance online.

Casares

Some 3 km west of Estepona, a winding road leads inland for 18 km to Casares, a lovely white town that attracts many tourists. Its whitewashed houses clothe the side of a hill which is capped by the ruins of a 13th-century **Moorish fortress** on Roman foundations, which was built in the time of Ibn al Jatib. The fort was also a centre of resistance against the French during the Peninsular War. Next to the fort is the **Iglesia de la Encarnación**, built in 1505 and with a brick *mudéjar* tower. There are majestic views from here along the whole coast and, on a good day, across to North Africa.

Casares is said to have derived its name from Julius Caesar, who may have been cured of his liver complaints by the sulphur springs at nearby Manilva. The 17th-century **Iglesia de San Sebastián**, which can be visited on the way to the fortress, is a simple whitewashed 17th-century building containing the image of the Virgen del Rosario del Campo. In the adjacent square is a statue of Blas Infante who was a native of Casares and leader of the Andalucían nationalist movement. He was executed by Falangists shortly after the start of the Civil War.

The **tourist office** ⓘ *C Carreras 46, T952-895521, winter Mon-Fri 1100-1430, 1600-1830, Sat 1100-1600, summer Mon-Sat 0900-1400,* is located in the house where Blas Infante was born, on the main road through town. They can provide details of a number of good circular walks that start from the main road just above the village.

From Casares, it is an exciting 20-minute drive to **Gaucín**, see page 60.

Listings Around Marbella

Where to stay

Benahavís

€€€€ Amanhavis Hotel
C Pilar 3, T952-856026,
www.amanhavis.com.
This hotel is a real one-off. The rooms are themed, ranging from a Moorish sultan's bedchamber to an astronomer's observatory. They vary substantially in facilities and price, but all are charmingly decorated. The restaurant here is excellent, specializing in fresh seasonal fare. Recommended.

Estepona
Book ahead for accommodation in Jul and Aug. There are numerous hotels, and you tend to get better rates via online hotel websites or travel agencies. Make sure you confirm the location;
'Estepona' can refer to a spot on the main road 5 km from town.

€ Hostal El Pilar
Plaza de las Flores 10, T952-800018,
www.hostalelpilar.es.
With a great location on the prettiest square in Estepona and a couple of minutes from the beach, this offers plenty of value. Decoration is simple, airy and cheerful, and the management are kindly. All rooms come with bathroom, and there are a few that sleep 4, good for families or groups.

Casares

€€ Hotel Rural Casares
C Copera 52, T952-895211.
Just off the plaza, this simple hotel has a rather old-fashioned feel but boasts some good views over the village.

Rooms are clean and well-priced, management is formally courteous, and a simple breakfast is included.

Restaurants

Estepona
Apart from the big hotels outside town, the main restaurants are around pedestrianized C Real, a block back from the beach, and C Terraza, which crosses it in the centre.

€€ Los Rosales
C Damas 12, T952-792945, www. restaurantelosrosales.com.
An excellent place in the centre, with high-quality fish given expert, and not too interventionist, treatment by the chef. Recommended.

Casares

€€ The Forge/Restaurante El Forjador
Ctra Casares Km 10, T952-895120, www. forgesrestaurant.com. Book ahead; opens for lunch Wed-Sun in winter and dinner Wed-Sat plus Sun lunch in summer.
Just above the road between Estepona and Casares, this hideaway among larch and cork trees offers a warm welcome, views, and a sweet dining area and indoor terrace. Some British classics take their place on the menu alongside lamb curry, Moroccan chicken and Spanish-influenced plates. Leave room for dessert.

Festivals

Ojén
1st week in Aug Fiesta de Flamenco.

Transport

Most of these bus services are run by **Portillo**, T902-450550, www.portillo. avanzabus.com.

Estepona
Estepona is served by regular daily buses along the coast in both directions.

Casares
The alternative route back to the coast at **Manilva** passes through attractive vineyards and limestone scenery, although the road surface is poor. There are 2 buses a day from **Estepona** to Casares.

North from
Málaga

Málaga's hinterland, the province's most interesting zone, is a world away from the busy coast. The main town in the north of the province is Antequera, which has a host of interesting monuments as well as a range of natural attractions. While the most direct route north is via the N331 *autovía*, a more enticing option for those with transport sends you northwest via the El Chorro region, gouged with gorges and redolent with curious local history.

Garganta del Chorro and Bobastro

a mighty ravine and Moorish ruins

Garganta del Chorro

Taking the Cártama road from Málaga, continue along the course of the Río Guadalhorce to **Pizarra**, and then to the white hilltop town of **Alora**. A 14th-century Alcazaba stands above it, largely in ruins; it now serves as Alora's cemetery. On the town's main square is the huge parish church of La Encarnación, built in the 18th century and said to be the province's second largest place of worship after Málaga's cathedral.

Just north of Alora fork right and after 12 km you will arrive at Garganta del Chorro, or Desfiladero de los Gaitanes, an impressive but narrow ravine cut into the limestone by the Río Guadalhorce. The striking railway cuts in and out of tunnels along the side of the gorge, which in some places is over 300 m deep. Also following the side of the gorge is a narrow path, **El Caminito del Rey**, which was built in the early 1920s and used by King Alfonso XIII when he opened the nearby hydroelectric works. It's a narrow, dramatic path of 3 km, recently rebuilt and reopened after years of dangerous neglect, and is scary but spectacular. An entry fee is due to be charged from mid-2015 onwards.

The gorge is a prime draw for rock climbers, who descend on El Chorro from all over Spain. There are many assisted climbing routes equipped with bolts or rings. Other activities you can arrange include canoeing and abseiling.

The hamlet of **El Chorro** is at the point the river is dammed, and it's where the train stops. It sits in magnificent surroundings; there's a hotel here, *casas rurales* nearby, and several hostels and campsites. It's also a popular lunch destination for malagueños at weekends.

★Bobastro

Six kilometres north of El Chorro, Bobastro is what remains of the stronghold of one of the most interesting characters in the history of Al-Andalus. Ibn Hafsun was a *muwallad* (from a family of Christian converts to Islam) who became a renegade after killing a neighbour in AD 879. Fleeing to North Africa, he returned after a year and set him up here, where he raised a ragtag army and became a real thorn in the side of the Córdoban rulers. Defeating various expeditions sent against him, he was captured in AD 883 and forced to join the army. After serving for a while, he deserted and returned to his fortress, where he rapidly started campaigning and conquering territory. At one point he held most of southern Andalucía with the help of various allies. He was never defeated and seems to have converted to Christianity; at any rate he built a church here. He died in AD 917, but his sons weren't able to keep hold of Bobastro for too long; it was retaken by Córdoba in AD 927.

Ibn Hafsun chose a wild, beautiful and highly defensible spot for his fortress, of which little remains atop the hill. Before reaching it, you pass the Mozarabic church in which later sources claim he was buried. It's a place of great beauty and solitude. It's in ruins, but a horseshoe arch has been preserved and the views are enchanting. Although Bobastro was once a sizeable town, scattered stone is all that remains.

Listings Garganta del Chorro and Bobastro

Where to stay

Garganta del Chorro
There are several *refugios* near the train station charging around €10-14 for a dorm bed. There's also a campsite.

€€€ Cortijo Valverde
Apt 47, Alora, T952-112979, www. cortijovalverde.com. Minimum 2-night stay.
A rural hotel set in olive and almond groves near El Chorro. Each cottage has its own terrace and superb views. There's a pool, the hotel makes an environmental effort and walking and other activities in the area can be arranged. Breakfast is included, and other meals are available.

€€ Complejo Turístico La Garganta
Bda El Chorro s/n, T952-495000, www.la garganta.com.

Dominating the hamlet, and offering spectacular views over the reservoir and gorge, this former flour mill is now a hotel. Attractive rooms and apartments are compact but fairly priced; it's more for a room with balcony. All have modern rustic decor; there's a pool, and the outdoor restaurant terrace buzzes with contented chatter during weekend lunches.

€ Finca La Campana
T626-963942, www.fincalacampana. com. Reception open 0900-1100, 1900-2100.
A hospitable base run by climbers 2 km from the railway station. They offer climbing, caving and mountain bike trips and have cosy double and family accommodation in a variety of cottages or in the *refugio*, where a dorm bed costs €12. You can also camp. All guests

have use of the kitchen and pool, and there's a shop. Mountain bikes, climbing gear and kayaks can be hired here. Recommended.

Garganta del Chorro

There are no buses to El Chorro, but 2 daily trains arrive from **Málaga** (40 mins). Both stop in **Alora**. One continues to **Ronda**, one to **Sevilla**.

Ardales and Carratraca

pretty hilltop settlement and spa

The main town in the region, Ardales is 10 km west of El Chorro. It's a pleasant place, capped by a ruined castle that was presumably also built by Ibn Hafsun. Below it is the church, **Nuestra Señora de los Remedios**, which is a mixture of the *mudéjar* and Baroque; from the former style it conserves a fine wooden ceiling. Also in town are a couple of museums, one dedicated to the **Cueva de Ardales** ⓘ *4 km outside of town, T952-458046.* Important Palaeolithic paintings decorate this cave, discovered in the early 19th century. The cave is closed to the public except by prior appointment, which you should arrange well in advance. If you read Spanish, the results of geological and archaeological investigations are summarized on www.cuevadeardales.com.

Some 5 km southeast of Ardales is **Carratraca,** famous for its sulphurous waters which were highly regarded back in Roman times. The village really took off in the 19th century when the despotic King Fernando VII built a mansion here for his personal use. Royal patronage made society sit up and take notice, and numerous famous visitors from all over Europe came here to take the waters, which, with a constant temperature of 18°C, is emphatically a summer-only pastime. There's a luxury spa hotel here, and in recent years, Carratraca has revived the performance of its ancient passion play, which takes place on Good Friday and Easter Saturday in the bullring, with a cast of over 100 villagers.

Listings Ardales and Carratraca

Where to stay

Ardales

€€ Posada del Conde
Pantano del Chorro 16-18, Ardales, T952-112411, www.hotel delconde.com.
This stately old building has been well converted into a comfortable hotel. It has high-quality rooms, with plenty of space and good bathrooms, and a restaurant serving generous and elaborate cuisine including hearty Castilian roasts.

Carratraca

€€€€ Villa Padierna
C Antonio Rioboo 11, Carratraca, T952-489542, villapadiernathermashotel.com.
This luxury spa hotel seeks to recreate the glory days – Roman, Moorish and 19th century – of taking the waters. The installations are magnificently attractive,

as is the building; try to nab a deal that includes spa treatments or meals.

Restaurants

Ardales
On and around the central Plaza de San Isidro are a handful of good tapas bars, including **El Mellizo**.

Transport

Ardales
There are 4 daily buses from **Málaga** to Ardales; these continue to **Ronda**.

Antequera and around

some of Europe's most impressive prehistoric dolmens

You know a town must be pretty old when even the Romans named it 'ancient place', or Antikaria. It's an excellent place to visit; on the city's edge stand three stunning prehistoric dolmens. The old town has numerous noble buildings of great interest, and the surrounding area offers tempting excursions to the dramatic rockscapes of El Torcal, the Lobo Park wolfery, and the flamingo lake of La Fuente de Piedra.

The dolmens are an obvious indication that the Antequera hilltop was an important prehistoric settlement, and the town's strategic position at the head of one of the easiest routes to the coast also appealed to the Romans. The Moors fortified the town with a citadel and, as part of the kingdom of Granada, Antequera didn't fall to the Christians until 1410. After becoming an important military base for assaults on the remaining Moorish possessions, the city grew in wealth in the 16th and 17th centuries, from which period most of its monuments date.

Sights

The centre of Antequera is Plaza San Sebastián, on which stands the **tourist office** ⓘ *C Encarnación 1, T952-702505, www.turismo.antequera.es, Mon-Sat 0930-1900, Sun 1000-1400*, which has helpful information on the town and area.

At the top of town, the **Arco de los Gigantes**, a triumphal arch built in 1585, gives on to the attractive Plaza de los Escribanos, by which stands the town's most impressive church, **Real Colegiata de Santa María la Mayor** ⓘ *Tue-Sat 1000-1900 (1030-1730 Oct-Apr), Sun 1030-1500, €3*, with a beautiful Renaissance façade worked on, among others, by the master Diego de Siloé in the mid-16th century. The spacious interior is now used for exhibitions and concerts and is a fine space with fat Ionic columns and a wooden ceiling. The cedarwood baldachin is a recent replica of the original. From the terrace beside the church, as well as stirring views, you can examine the excavated **Roman baths** below you.

The hillside above the church is covered with a peaceful hedged garden stretching up to the **Alcazaba** ⓘ *Tue-Sat 1000-1900 (1030-1730 Oct-Apr), Sun 1030-1500, €6 including Santa María la Mayor*, the remains of the Moorish fortress. The best-preserved feature is the **Torre del Homenaje** (keep) from the 13th century.

The castle has been comprehensively restored (actually, completely rebuilt in places, which has raised various authenticity questions) and is an atmospheric spot. From the hilltop you look across to the curiously shaped hill known as the **Peña de los Enamorados** (Lovers' Hill), from which it is said that a pair of star-crossed Moorish lovers threw themselves when their union was prohibited.

Antequera's rich archaeological heritage is represented in the **Museo de la Ciudad de Antequera** ① *Plaza del Coso Viejo, May-Sep Tue-Fri 0930-1400, 1900-2100, Sat 0930-1400, 1800-2100, Sun 1000-1400, Oct-Apr Tue-Fri 0930-1400, 1630-1830, Sat 0930-1400, 1600-1900, Sun 1000-1400, €3*, near the Plaza San Sebastián. Set in a *palacio* dating from the Renaissance, it's a display of mixed quality, but has some outstanding pieces. The pride and joy of the museum is a famous Roman bronze statue dating from the first century AD. A life-sized depiction of a naked boy known as Efebo, it's a fine work. There are also some high-quality Roman mosaics in the museum. Another sculpture worth a look is a beautifully rendered St Francis, which is attributed to Alonso Cano.

There's another museum nearby, in the **Convento de las Carmelitas Descalzas** ① *Plaza de las Descalzas s/n, T606-855792, Tue-Fri 1030-1400, 1700-2000, Sat 0900-1230, 1700-2000, Sun 0900-1230, plus 1700-2000 summer, closed Jul, guided tours on the half hour, €3.30*, the order founded by Teresa of Avila. The visit is by guided tour and as worthwhile for the building as for the artworks, although a Luca Giordano depiction of Teresa herself is a fine work.

Antequera is full of other churches; in fact, although it likes to call itself the Athens of Andalucía, Rome might be (marginally) more accurate. Among them is the **Iglesia del Carmen** ① *May-Sep Mon-Fri 0900-1400, 1630-1900, Sat-Sun 1000-1330, 1700-1900, Oct-Apr Tue-Fri 1100-1330, 1630-1745, Sat-Sun 1100-1400, €2*, which has a *mudéjar* ceiling but is most notable for its excellent wooden *retablo*. Dating from the 18th century, it was carved by Antonio Primo in incredible size and detail; it's decorated with a wealth of scrolls, volutes and cherubs, as well as figures of popes, archbishops, John the Baptist and other prophets. Also look out for the pretty organ in the gallery and some ornate fresco work in one of the side chapels.

On the Plaza del Portichuelo, look out for the highly unusual arched brick façade of the small chapel, the **Tribuna del Portichuelo**. On the same square is the church of **Santa María de Jesús**, a bright white Baroque creation.

★Dolmens
All dolmens Tue-Sat 1000-1830 (summer until 2030), Sun 1000-1700. Free.

The highlight of any visit to Antequera will be a visit to these hugely impressive and moving monuments. They are megalithic in the true sense of the word, consisting of vast slabs of stone, the largest of which weighs a massive 180 tons. The stones were dragged over 1 km from a nearby quarry. After erecting the upright stones, earth ramps were constructed to manoeuvre the covering slabs into place. There are three dolmens, dating from the Chalcolithic period; they were built as burial chambers, presumably for important chiefs.

The adjacent **Menga** and **Viera** dolmens are about 1 km from the centre of town. From Plaza San Sebastián, walk down Calle Encarnación past the tourist office, carry on straight ahead, and follow the road (now Calle Carrera) left. Eventually you'll reach the entrance to the dolmen area on your left. You access the dolmens through an interpretation centre that provides some context. Menga, the oldest of them, dates from approximately 2500 BC, and is an eerily atmospheric chamber roofed with vast stone slabs. Recently, a deep well has been discovered at one end of the chamber. At the entrance, the staff on duty will point out the faint engravings in the portal. On Midsummer's Day, the rising sun shines directly into the chamber from behind the Peña de los Enamorados, clearly of ritual significance. The Viera dolmen dates from some five centuries later and has an access corridor leading to a smaller burial chamber.

El Romeral dolmen stands a further couple of kilometres out past the Menga and Viera dolmens; turn left when you reach the major intersection (head for Córdoba/Sevilla), then turn left after crossing the railway line. It dates to around 1800 BC and presents a very different aspect, with smaller corbelled stones being used to wall the access chamber and half-domed burial chamber, which is entered through a doorway.

El Torcal

This massive chunk of limestone, 16 km south of Antequera, has been weathered into rugged and surreal sculptural karstic formations and is a memorable place to visit, although preferably on a weekday when it's less crowded. The bulk of the massif is a *parque natural* and a **visitor centre** ⓘ *T952-702505, daily 1000-1700 (1900 summer)*, atop it has exhibitions on the formations and wildlife; there's also an audiovisual presentation and café. From here, there's a short path leading to a stunning viewpoint and, from the centre's car park, two marked walking trails of approximately 45 minutes and two hours' duration. Spring is an excellent time to explore El Torcal, as the grey rocky zone is enlivened by a riot of colourful wildflowers.

The closest town is **Villanueva de la Concepción**, 18 km southwest of Antequera and served by buses from there and Málaga. The tourist office in Antequera can arrange a taxi to take you to the visitor centre, wait for you to do the trail, and take you back to town.

Lobo Park

Ctra Antequera–Alora Km 16, T952-031107, www.lobopark.com, daily 1000-1800, tours 1100, 1300, 1500, 1630, €11, children €7.

An intriguing spot to visit in easy striking distance of Antequera, this wolf park houses a variety of lupine residents rescued from the wild or captivity. The tour visits the enclosures of several different packs – Iberian, timber, European, and Arctic wolves are all present. There's heaps of information – enquire ahead if you want an English-speaking guide – and it's fascinating to see the packs' strict hierarchies, plus the group 'bonding' behaviour after being fed. There's a good ecological vibe here, and the visit also includes a look at some domestic animals –

a hit with the kids, but also great to see some animals rescued from the wild, including a pair of foxes who literally jump for joy when their handler approaches. A few nights a month from May to October you can pre-book a visit to hear the wolves howling in unison; an eerie moonlit sound. It includes dinner; check the website for dates.

Laguna de la Fuente de Piedra
Twenty kilometres northwest of Antequera, this large saltwater lake is one of Europe's most important breeding grounds for the greater flamingo. The loveably awkward pinkish birds arrive early in the year to rear their chicks and hang around until the water level drops in summer, usually in late July or August. There are dozens of other waterbird species present, including avocets, terns and the rare white-headed duck. There's an **information centre** ⓘ *T952-111715, Wed-Sun 1000-1400, 1600-1800 (1800-2000 Apr-Sep)*, by the lake that hires binoculars and provides birdwatching advice.

Nearby, **El Refugio del Burrito** ⓘ *T952-735077, www.elrefugiodelburrito.com, 1000-1800, free*, rescues donkeys and mules from across Europe and brings them here to rehabilitate and enjoy retirement in the Andalucían sunshine. It's great for kids and entry is free, but the organization relies on donations, so you may want to sponsor one of the gentle long-eared beasts for €15 per year.

Archidona
Some 15 km east of Antequera lies this once strategic town. Occupied by the Iberians, the Romans and the Moors and defended by a hilltop castle, it was captured by Christian forces in 1462. Later it was the chief town of the Counts of Ureña and the Dukes of Osuna.

Today, it is a backwater, bypassed by both the main road and the *autovía* to Granada. Its pride and joy, however, is Plaza Ochavada, a late 18th-century octagonal square, surrounded by buildings using ornamental brickwork and stone. It's a lovely space, and on it is the **tourist office** ⓘ *T952-716479, www.archidona.org*. Further up the hill, a palm-shaded plaza is home to the Casa Consistorial, which boasts a beautiful carved façade. It now houses the municipal museum.

Listings Antequera and around

Where to stay

€€€ **Parador de Antequera**
C García de Olmo s/n, T952-840261, www.parador.es.
The town's modern parador is near the bullring on the edge of town and offers quiet comfort. There's a pool and pleasant gardens; the rooms have polished floors and large beds.

€ **Hotel Plaza San Sebastián**
Plaza San Sebastián 4, T952-844239, www.hotelplaza sansebastian.com.
Centrally located, this friendly hotel has recently renovated modern rooms with a/c, heating and good bathrooms.

A sound choice lacking character but good value.

Laguna de la Fuente de Piedra
Camping

Camping Fuente Piedra
Camino de la Rábita s/n, T952-735294, www.campingfuentedepiedra.com.
A good base for flamingo-watchers, this well-equipped campsite is close to the lake and open all year. As well as tent and van sites, there are bungalows and rooms available. Pool and bar/restaurant.

Restaurants

€€ Mesón El Escribano
Plaza de los Escribanos 11, T952-706533.
This popular restaurant has a terrace looking out at the collegiate church and specializes in local dishes such as *porra*, a thick tomato cold soup similar to *salmorejo*.

Bars and clubs

Manolo Bar
C Calzada 14, T952-841015.
Open 1700-late.
With a Wild West theme, it serves a big mix of Antequera folk, coffee, tapas and mixed drinks late into the night.

Transport

Bus
Antequera is well served by buses from **Málaga**, which run almost hourly (1 hr) from the bus station, a 15-min walk north of Plaza San Sebastián. There are 5 daily buses to **Granada**, and 5 to **Sevilla** via **Osuna**. There are also connections to **Córdoba** and other Andalucían cities.

Train
The train station is 1.5 km north of the town centre. There are 3 daily trains to **Ronda** (1 hr 10 mins) and services to **Sevilla** (4 a day, 1 hr 50 mins), **Granada** and **Algeciras**. Regular fast trains between Málaga and Córdoba stop at Antequera–Santa Ana station, 17 km west of town.

Laguna de la Fuente de Piedra
There are 3 buses daily from **Antequera** to Fuente de Piedra village.

Archidona
6-7 daily buses between **Antequera** and Archidona (20 mins), continuing to **Granada**.

Ronda

★"There is one town that would be better than Aranjuez to see your first bullfight in if you were only going to see one and that is Ronda. That is where you should go if you ever go to Spain on a honeymoon or if you ever bolt with anyone." Ernest Hemingway, *Death in the Afternoon*.

The cradle of bullfighting as we know it, Ronda features high on the must-see list of many visitors to Andalucía because of its picturesque whitewashed streets and, most spectacularly, its position straddling a deep gorge that separates the old and new parts of town. The gorge is spanned by the Puente Nuevo, a late 18th-century bridge that crosses 80 m above the stream below.

These attractions mean that it's overrun with tourists in peak season; to really appreciate the town you should spend a night or two here, as most people come on day trips and by six in the evening the tour buses have rolled back to the coast. Pack a thick coat if you plan to visit in winter.

Plaza de España and Puente Nuevo

It's likely that you'll make this your first port of call in Ronda, as looking down into the gorge has a magnetic appeal. The plaza itself is dominated by the former town hall, now a parador. After pondering for a moment what idiot allowed a McDonald's to be opened next to it, move over to the Tajo and look down 80 m or so into the narrow gorge.

The Puente Nuevo was built in the late 18th century and designed by José Martín de Aldehuela. Legend says that he died falling into the gorge while carving the date on the bridge, but this is in fact untrue – he died in Málaga several years later. The stones were raised on pulleys from the bottom of the Tajo. Within the bridge itself is an **interpretation centre** ① *Plaza de España s/n, T649-965338, Mon-Fri 1000-1800 or 1900, Sat and Sun 1000-1500, €2,* in what used to be a small prison. Apart from the knowledge that you're standing over the ravine, there's little worthwhile here.

Plaza de Toros

C Virgen de la Paz s/n, T952-874132. Daily 1000-1900 or 2000 in summer, €6.50, with audioguide €8.

One of the country's oldest, the Ronda bullring has a special appeal to lovers of tauromachy, for it was here that the rules for modern bullfighting were laid down by the Romero clan. While admission isn't cheap, if you have an interest in such things, it's well worth a visit. Apart from the thrill of walking out on to the arena itself, there's a museum with all sorts of memorabilia. You can also visit the stables, and, most interestingly, the bull pens, with their complex system of lifting gates operated from the safety of above.

Most of the other sights are across in the old town, but it's worth seeking out the **Templete de la Virgen de los Dolores**, also known as Los Ahorcados, on Calle Santa Cecilia. Built in the 18th century, it's a small chapel with a highly unusual façade. The Ionic columns

Ronda

In the collapse of the Córdoba caliphate, Ronda was seized by a Berber general and became its own *taifa* state before being annexed by Sevilla in 1066. Ronda wasn't reconquered by the Christians until 1485, when it was taken by forces under Fernando, the Catholic monarch. Always a centre for resistance and bandit activity, the Ronda area held out strongly in the 19th century against the invading French forces, leading villagers to chant 'Napoleón, Napoleón, conquistaste toda España, pero no pudiste entrar en la tierra de las castañas' (Napoleon, Napoleon, you conquered all of Spain, but you never could enter the land of the chestnuts).

Later, the town was popularized by Romantic travellers and became a haunt of artists and writers. Gustav Doré, Rainer Maria Rilke and Ernest Hemingway are among those who spent much time here. In the Civil War, many right-wingers were brutally murdered and the town shared its resources along a strict socialist system; reprisals after the Nationalist takeover were also fierce.

are supported by strange birdmen and other figures, a product of late-Baroque mannerism influenced by Latin-American imagery.

Ciudad Vieja

Known simply as La Ciudad, the old part of Ronda is a tight knot of small streets and white houses, including several noble *palacios* and churches. A stretch of the city walls still encircles part of the area, beyond which extend green fields and the mountains of the sierra.

After crossing the bridge over the chasm, take a quick left and you'll soon come to the **Casa del Rey Moro** ⓘ *Barrio de Padre Jesús s/n, T952-187200, daily 1000-1900, €4*. This evocatively faded mansion (also known as La Mina and Jardines de Forestier) with jutting wooden eaves was built in the 18th century over Moorish foundations. The principal attraction here is an impressive staircase hewn 80 m downwards through the rock to the river below. Some scholars say its function was merely so that slaves could fetch water for their Moorish master, but its real purpose is likely to have been as a sally-port in times of siege; legend attributes its construction to the king Abomelic. There are 232 steps down to the river, and they are slippery and steep. Once you're down you can admire the blue-green water from a tranquil small platform and look up at the town above. A fine landscaped garden is the other feature of the (slightly overpriced) attraction.

On exiting the Casa del Rey Moro, you will enjoy the fine views of the town and countryside. Below is an old entrance gate into the city, which commemorates Felipe V. A short distance beyond, following the river away from town, are the 14th-century **Baños Arabes (Arab baths)** ⓘ *Cuesta de Santo Domingo s/n, T656-950937, Mon-Fri 1000-1800 (1900 summer), Sat and Sun 1000-1500, €3*, preserving brick arches and star-shaped skylights.

Ronda

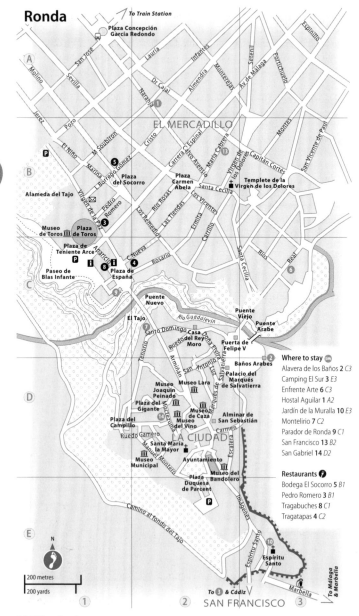

To Train Station

Plaza Concepción
García Redondo

El Mercadillo

Plaza del Socorro

Alameda del Tajo

Museo de Toros

Plaza de Toros

Plaza de Teniente Arce

Paseo de Blas Infante

Plaza de España

Plaza Carmen Abela

Templete de la Virgen de los Dolores

Puente Nuevo

El Tajo

Puente Viejo

Puente Árabe

Casa del Rey Moro

Puerta de Felipe V

Baños Árabes

Palacio del Marqués de Salvatierra

Museo Joaquín Peinado

Museo Lara

Plaza del Gigante

Museo de Caza

Museo del Vino

Alminar de San Sebastián

Plaza del Campillo

Santa María la Mayor

Museo Municipal

Ayuntamiento

Museo del Bandolero

Plaza Duquesa de Parcent

LA CIUDAD

Espíritu Santo

To **3** & Cádiz

SAN FRANCISCO

To Málaga & Marbella

N

200 metres

200 yards

Where to stay 🛏
Alavera de los Baños 2 *C3*
Camping El Sur 3 *E3*
Enfrente Arte 6 *C3*
Hostal Aguilar 1 *A2*
Jardín de la Muralla 10 *E3*
Montelirio 7 *C2*
Parador de Ronda 9 *C1*
San Francisco 13 *B2*
San Gabriel 14 *D2*

Restaurants 🍴
Bodega El Socorro 5 *B1*
Pedro Romero 3 *B1*
Tragabuches 8 *C1*
Tragatapas 4 *C2*

Just above the Puerta de Felipe V is the **Palacio del Marqués de Salvatierra**, one of the more impressive of Ronda's many elegant buildings. Its 18th-century Baroque façade has been recently restored, and features four columns carved with caryatid-like figures, in this case apparently native American inspired. Outside is a stone *crucero*.

Following this street along, you'll reach a small tower, the **Alminar de San Sebastián**, a former minaret of one of the town's many mosques. It's been capped by a later belfry but still preserves most of its original structure, including a horseshoe-arched window.

Near here, two grand and unusual buildings face each other across Plaza Duquesa de Parcent. The collegiate church of **Santa María la Mayor** ⓘ *Plaza Duquesa de Parcent s/n, T952-874048, daily 1000-1800 (2000 summer), closed Sun 1230-1400 €4*, was once Ronda's principal mosque. Converted into a church by Fernando, the Catholic Monarch, it retains little of its Moorish origins apart from an inscribed archway, the *mihrab* and the minaret, converted into a bell tower. Most striking is its double gallery looking out on to the square. The interior is mostly a blend of late Gothic and Renaissance arching; there's a fine elaborate choir, some poor frescoes, and an inlaid Churrigueresque *retablo*. Upstairs, behind the galleries, is an exhibition of polychrome sculpture.

On the same square are the long arcades of the **Ayuntamiento**, perhaps reminiscent of a row of shops for good reason, as it has been suggested that was once a Moorish market.

Beyond here, the Ciudad comes to an end in the Barrio de San Francisco, which has a well-preserved section of walls and a fine sandstone-block church in **Iglesia del Espíritu Santo**. A gate leads out through the walls towards the countryside beyond.

Back at Plaza Duquesa, head east to the **Museo Municipal** ⓘ *Plaza Mondragón s/n, T952-870818, www.museoderonda.es, Mon-Fri 1000-1800 (1900 summer), Sat and Sun 1000-1500, €3*, which is set in the Palacio de Mondragón, one of Ronda's most beautiful mansions. The building alone is worth the price of admission; it centres around two patios, the first with red arches and a well, the second with a wooden gallery and eaves, as well as colourful tilework. There's also a Moorish-style garden. The collection is a mixture of displays: the flora and fauna of the Sierra de los Nieves; a reconstruction of a late Bronze Age hut with thatched roof on stone foundations; of a cave; and a prehistoric metalworking furnace. One of the most important pieces is a seventh-century BC mould for making swords. There's also a resumé of Muslim funerary customs and a collection of Moorish gravestones.

There are several other museums in the Ciudad Vieja. The **Museo Lara** ⓘ *C Armiñán 29, T952-871263, www.museolara.org, daily 1100-2000 (1900 winter), €4*, could be described as a collection of collections, with a bizarre range of objects housed in yet another attractive *palacio*. There are swords, opera glasses, sewing machines, torture implements, witchcraft displays and typewriters among numerous other curios. There are flamenco shows here on spring and summer evenings. Nearby, the **Centro de Interpretación del Vino** ⓘ *C González Campos 2, T952 879 735, www.bodegaslasangrederonda.es, Mon-Thu and Sat 1030-1900 (2030*

ON THE ROAD

Los toros

The bullfight, or *corrida*, is an emblem of Spanish culture, a reminder of when Roman gladiators fought wild beasts in amphitheatres. It is emphatically not a sport (the result is a given) but a ritual; a display of courage by both animal and human. While to outside observers it can seem as if the bull is being tortured and humiliated, that is not the way many Spaniards perceive it, though there is an ever-increasing lobby against it in the country.

The myth that bullfighting aficionados are a bloodthirsty lot should be dispelled. Nobody likes to see a *torero* hurt, a less-than-clean kill, or overuse of the *pic*. What keeps many people going is that all-too-rare sublime fight, where the *matador* is breathtakingly daring, and the bull strong and courageous.

The fighting bull, or *toro de lidia*, is virtually a wild animal reared in vast ranches where human contact is minimal. It enters the ring when it is about four years old, and weighs about 500 kg.

In a standard bullfight there are six bulls and three *matadores*, who fight two each. The fights take 15 minutes each, so a standard *corrida* lasts about two hours, usually starting in the late afternoon. The fight is divided into three parts, or *tercios*. In the first part, the bull emerges and is then played with the cape by the *matador*, who judges its abilities and tendencies. The bull is then induced to charge a mounted *picador*, who meets it with a sharp lance which is dug into the bull's neck muscles as it tries to toss the horse. Although the horses are thankfully padded these days, it's the most difficult part of the fight to enjoy or comprehend and *picadores* (following the *matador*'s orders) frequently overdo it with the lance, tiring, hurting and dispiriting the animal.

summer), Fri 1100-1800, Sun 1100-1530, €5, is a bodega with a pretty patio; the tour includes a taste of one wine; for an extra fee you can taste more Andalucían drops; the **Museo de Caza** is devoted to hunting, while the **Museo del Bandolero** pays homage to the famous bandits of the region. Lastly, the **Museo Joaquín Peinado** is a gallery with works by that *rondeño* painter of the Paris school.

Around Ronda

The ruins of **Acinipo** ⓘ *Ctra MA-449 s/n, T952-041452, Wed-Sun 1000-1500, opening times are changeable, so ring ahead, free,* also known as **Ronda la Vieja**, lie 12 km northwest of Ronda off the Sevilla road. An important Roman town in its day (the first century AD was its zenith), it later declined as Ronda's fortunes rose. Sprawled across a hilltop, most of the ruins are fragmentary, but what makes the visit worthwhile is the massive theatre with views across the sierra. There are also remains of earlier Iberian and Phoenician structures. Not much further is the strange and beautiful town of **Setenil de las Bodegas**.

Cueva de la Pileta ⓘ *Benaoján, T952-167343, daily 1000-1300, 1600-1700 (1800 summer), entry by guided tour on the hour in groups of up to 25, 1 hr,* an important

The second *tercio* involves the placing of three pairs of darts, or *banderillas*, in the bull's neck muscles, to further tire it so that the head is carried low enough to allow the *matador* to reach the point where the sword should go in. The placing of the *banderillas* is usually rapid and skilful, done on foot, occasionally by the *matador* himself.

The last part is the *tercio de la muerte*, the third of death. The *matador* faces the bull with a *muleta* (small cape) and a sword. He passes it a few times then positions himself for the kill. After profiling (turning side on and pointing the sword at the bull), he aims for a point that should kill the bull instantly. But this rarely happens; there are often a few attempts, with the animal wounded and gushing blood, and then a *descabello* (coup de grace), where the spinal cord is severed below the base of the skull.

If the spectators have been impressed by the bullfighter's performance, they stand and wave their handkerchiefs at the president of the ring, who may then award one or two ears and, for exceptional performances, the tail as well. These are then chopped off the animal and paraded around the ring by the fighter, who will be thrown hats and wineskins as gestures of appreciation. Meanwhile, the dead bull has been dragged out in a flurry of dust by mules; if it has fought well, it will be applauded out of the ring.

Andalucía justly claims to be the cradle of bullfighting, and rings at El Puerto de Santa María, Ronda and Sevilla are among the most prestigious in Spain. The famous Ronda school developed the structure of the fight as we see it today. Another type of bullfight is the *corrida de rejones*, where skilled riders fight the bull from horseback atop highly trained mounts; a combination of skill and showmanship.

cave 20 km southwest of Ronda, was discovered in 1905 by a local farmer. On following a stream of bats in the hope of collecting some of their dung as fertilizer, he came across a series of prehistoric paintings. The cave is 2 km long and further exploration has revealed a large quantity of art in various different chambers. While the limestone formations aren't the most spectacular you've ever seen, the visit is fascinating, and guided by a descendant of the original farmer. Commentary, in Spanish, and limited English, is intelligent and humorous. The oldest paintings date from the Palaeolithic and range from 12,000 to 30,000 years old. You can see a horsehead, bulls, goats, a fish, and a seal. The oldest probably represents the earliest phase of Cro-Magnon presence in Europe. There are also Neolithic paintings; mostly geometric patterns and abstract forms, but also what appears to be a form of calendar. It's all the better for being able to peer at these paintings by lantern light before the inevitable interpretation centre is built. To get there, take a left off the A-574 (Sevilla) road not far below Ronda; it's signposted Benaoján. When you get to Benaoján, head through the village, then take a sharp left as you leave it on the other side. The cave is 5 km along this road; bat-phobes should stay in the car.

As well as the excursions listed above, the white towns of Cádiz province, including Grazalema, are close at hand.

Ronda to Gaucín

One of the province's more spectacular drives heads from Ronda southwest towards Algeciras through a succession of whitewashed hilltop villages with a distinctly Moorish ambience. **Atajate**, some 18 km from Ronda, is typical, with a high 19th-century church and perspectives over olive groves, grapevines and chestnut woods. **Benadalid** boasts a castle that was strategically crucial in the Reconquista, while larger **Benalauría** and **Algatocín** have several fine buildings amid their narrow streets. The most interesting of the towns, **Gaucín**, makes a tempting rural base and is dominated by its ruined fortress on a rocky crag high over town. From Gaucín, you can cross a valley via a spectacular road to the pretty town of Casares, near Estepona on the Costa del Sol, see page 43. A 13-km detour south from Algatocín, Genalguacil seems like another typical village from afar, until you arrive and find its streets, parks and plazas stocked full of sculptures of every type imaginable, a legacy of a biennial gathering of artists in the village. It's well worth the detour to see it.

Listings Ronda *map p56*

Tourist information

Regional office
Plaza de España 1, T952-169311. Mon-Fri 0900-1930, Sat and Sun 0930-1500.
Ronda's municipal office (Paseo Blas Infante s/n, T952-187119, Mon-Fri 1000-1800, Sat 1000-1400, 1500-1700, Sun 1000-1430) is near the regional one next to the bullring. Both offices have a wide range of information in several languages on the town and area. There is also a useful tourism website, www.turismoderonda.es.

Where to stay

€€€€ Parador de Ronda
Plaza de España s/n, T952-877500, www. parador.es.
Set in the former town hall on the very edge of the Tajo by the Puente Nuevo bridge, this parador has one of the most memorable locations of any Andalucían hotel. While its public areas still suffer from a municipal feel, the rooms are excellent, with comfortable furniture, polished floorboards, plenty of space and big beds. The pricier ones have balconies overlooking the gorge, and it's hard to beat the hotel pool, which is right on the lip of it.

€€€ Hotel Jardín de la Muralla
C Espíritu Santo 13, T952-872764, www. jardindela muralla.com.
A charming hotel set around a central patio, it has large, light rooms that are cheerfully furnished with curios and pictures. There's a lounge with a piano and a garden terrace. Breakfast is included. Good value.

€€€ Hotel Montelirio
C Tenorio 8, T952-873855, www. hotelmontelirio.com.

Close to the bridge, and with rooms and spacious junior suites offering views (rooms without a view are only €16 less, so you might as well), this boutique hotel impresses on many levels, not least for its welcoming management. The more than decent restaurant has a terrace perched right on the edge of the ravine, and there's also a small pool. Recommended.

€€ Alavera de los Baños
C San Miguel s/n, T952-879143, www. alaveradelosbanos.com.
Delightful small hotel with an organically minded restaurant, located between the town walls and the Baños Arabes. Rooms are charmingly and tastefully decorated and you'll get a warm welcome from the owners. Relaxing garden with a pool. Breakfast included. Recommended.

€€ Hotel Enfrente Arte
C Real 40, T952-879088, www. enfrentearte.com.
This stylish and friendly hotel is painted throughout in bright pastel colours that define the funky mood of the place. The rooms are cheerful and comfortable and vary in size and price; some have views. There's a pool, pool table and internet access and, with a generous breakfast/brunch buffet and all beverages included, it's a delight. Recommended.

€€ Hotel San Francisco
C María Cabrera 18, T952-873299, www. hotelsanfrancisco-ronda.com.
This well-run, central choice has a variety of rooms with colourful bedspreads and padded headboards. They are excellent value, have plenty of light and very good bathrooms, as well as TV, heating and a/c. Rates include breakfast. Recommended for decent sleeping at a low price.

€€ Hotel San Gabriel
C Marqués de Moctezuma 19, T952-190392, www.hotelsan gabriel.com.
Beautifully restored and located townhouse run with real love by 3 siblings who grew up in it. A tastefully old-fashioned lounge has bookcases and old sofas. The rooms are elegant; the larger ones have colourful screens to make the space a bit more intimate. Bathrooms and facilities are top-grade without detracting from the old-world charm. Easy street parking nearby. Excellent continental breakfast for a little extra. Highly recommended.

€ Hostal Aguilar/Doña Carmen
C Naranja 28, T952-871994, www. hostaldonacarmen.com.
Modernized *hostal* with good clean rooms and heating, run by a friendly family. There's another section with older, shabbier rooms that are gradually being renovated; these have shared bathroom and are fine value in summer but iceboxes in winter.

Camping

Camping El Sur
Ctra A369, Km 2, 2 km out of town on the Algeciras road, T952-875939, www. campingelsur.com. Open all the year.
This excellent campsite has a pool, bar, restaurant and tidy modern bungalows.

Ronda to Gaucín

€€ Hotel La Fructuosa
C Convento 67, Gaucín, T617-692784, www.lafructuosa.com.
This excellent rural hotel is an appetizing place right in the heart of pretty Gaucín, 36 km southwest of Ronda, and a base for walking and driving exploration of the surrounding

hills. All the rooms are different, offering great views and decorated with exquisite modern rural style. Facilities include a fabulous roof terrace; the included breakfast and the warm personal service also make this a standout.

Restaurants

Many of Ronda's restaurants are tourist traps. Avoid most of the ones along C Nueva.

€€€ Pedro Romero
C Virgen de la Paz 18, T952-871110, www.rpedroromero.com.
The best of the restaurants along the main street near the bullring and predictably decorated with taurine memorabilia. Although it sees its fair share of tourists, it can't be faulted on quality. The bull's tail is particularly good, but anything with a local flavour is recommended. The lunchtime *menú* is decent but the à la carte is more memorable.

€€€ Tragabuches
C José Aparicio 1, T952-878447, www.tragabuches.com.
With an attractive modern dining area with big plate-glass windows looking out over the gardens by the bullring, this restaurant usually wins the foodies' vote as Ronda's most creative. The menu is a small one and changes often. The prices are high for Spain, but OK for the quality on offer; try anything with local *setas* (wild mushrooms). The best way to eat here is to take the pricey but memorable degustation menu.

€€ Tragatapas
C Nueva 4, T952-877209, www.facebook.com/tragatapas.
The delicious fare at this central tapas bar features plenty of innovation, with ox *tataki* taking its place alongside salmon with vanilla and lime or fried squid with broad beans. Recommended.

€ Bodega El Socorro
C Molina 4, T651-746099, www.facebook.com/bodegasocorro.
Just off Plaza del Socorro, this warm and busy bar is decorated with farm tools. The tapas are excellent; try the spinach croquettes, prawn and bacon brochettes or the cold pasta salad.

Festivals

Early Sep Ronda's main fiesta, named in honour of **Pedro Romero** is celebrated with bullfights in 18th-century costumes. There's also a flamenco festival as part of it.

What to do

Bike hire
CycleRonda, *C Juan José de Puya 21, T952-083553, www.cycleronda.com.* Hires bikes at €15 a day.
Pangea, *Pasaje Cayetano 10, T630-562705, www.pangeacentral.com.* Offers outdoor activities in the surrounding area; check website for details.

Bullfighting
You'll need to be here in mid-May for the *feria* or in early Sep for the fiestas. Book tickets on T952-876967 (fiesta box office opens 1 Jul).

Transport

Ronda's bus and train stations are both on Av de Andalucía on the northern edge of the new town, a 10- to 15-min walk from Plaza de España.

Bus

There are 4 to 10 daily buses to **Málaga** (2 hrs), some direct. **Sevilla** is served 3-5 times daily (2 hrs 30 mins), and there are a couple of daily buses to **Marbella** and **Fuengirola**. Other destinations include **Grazalema** and **Ubrique** (2 a day, none on Sun), **Cádiz** via **Arcos de la Frontera** and **Jerez** 5 times daily, 1 to **Algeciras** via **Gaucín** and **Jimena de la Frontera**, and 6 to nearby **Setenil** (4 on Sat, none on Sun).

Train

Ronda is on the train line running from **Algeciras** to **Granada** via **Jimena de la Frontera** and **Antequera**. There are 3 daily trains to **Granada**, 2 hrs 30 mins, and 5 to **Algeciras**, 1 hr 45 mins, as well as connections to Bobadilla and then **Córdoba**, **Málaga**, **Madrid** and **Sevilla**.

Background
Andalucía

History

Spain's proximity to Africa meant that Andalucía was one of Europe's frontlines for migrating hominids from the south. Discoveries near Burgos, in Spain's north attest that prehistoric humans inhabited the peninsula 1.3 million years ago; these are the oldest known hominid remains in Western Europe. Andalucía was a likely entry point.

One of the most important prehistoric European finds was discovered in **Gibraltar**; the finding of a woman's skull in one of the enclave's numerous caves was the first evidence of Neanderthals. The fossilized cranium has been dated to some 60,000 years.

While these fragments from an inconceivably distant past do little more than tantalize, there is substantial archaeological evidence of extensive occupation of Andalucía in the Upper Palaeolithic period. Several caves across the region have painting dating from this period, such as **La Pileta** near Ronda, and **Nerja** on the Málaga coast. Although not as sophisticated as the roughly contemporary works at Altamira in northern Spain, the depictions of horses, deer, fish and other animals are almost 20,000 years old and give a valuable insight into the lives of these early groups.

In 6000 BC, waves of immigration in the Almería area seem to have to ushered southern Spain rapidly into the Neolithic era. The Granada archaeological museum has some stunning finds from the **Cueva de los Murciélagos** in the south of the province, where burial goods include finely worked gold jewellery and some happily preserved woven *esparto* objects. From the same period are a new series of cave paintings at sites such as the **Cueva de los Letreros** near Vélez Blanco; one of the motifs here is the *Indalo*, a stick figure that was still used in the region until relatively recently as protection against evil spirits.

Around the middle of the third millennium, megalithic architecture began to appear in the form of dolmens, stone burial chambers whose most impressive exemplars are the massive structures at **Antequera**. At around the same time, the site of **Los Millares** in Almería province reveals a thriving and expanding society with an economy based on animal husbandry and working of copper; there is clear evidence of some form of contact with other Mediterranean peoples.

The Almería area is in a favoured geographical position for this type of cultural interchange, and it is no coincidence that the peninsula's first Bronze Age culture, known as **Agaric**, emerged in this region. Although almost nothing remains of the hilltop settlements themselves, excavations have retrieved bronze artefacts of a high technical standard and material that suggests extensive sea trading networks around the beginning of 2000 BC.

Around the turn of the first millennium, the face of the region was changing significantly. The people named as **Iberians** in later texts, and probably of local origin, inhabited the area and were joined by some **Celts**, although these peoples predominantly settled in the north of the peninsula. The Iberians had two distinct languages, unrelated to the Indo-European family, and benefited significantly from the arrival of another group, the **Phoenicians**.

These master sailors and merchants from the Levant set up many trading stations on the Andalucían coast. These included modern Huelva, Málaga and Cádiz; the latter, which they named **Gadir**, was possibly founded around 1100 BC, which would make it Western Europe's most venerable city. The Phoenicians set about trading with the Iberians, and began extensive mining operations, extracting gold, silver and copper from Andalucía's richly endowed soils.

Profitable contact with this maritime superpower led to the emergence of the wealthy local **Tartessian** civilization. Famed in classical sources as a mystical region where demigods walked streets paved with gold, precious little is actually known about this culture. Although they developed writing, it is undeciphered. Although it seems that they had an efficiently controlled society, no site worthy of being identified as the capital, Tartessos, has been excavated. Seemingly based in the region around the Guadalquivir valley, including in such settlements as Carmona, Niebla and Huelva, the Tartessians were highly skilled craftsmen; the Carambolo hoard found in Sevilla province consists of astonishingly intricate and beautiful gold jewellery.

Towards the end of the sixth century BC, the Tartessian culture seems to disappear and Iberian settlements appear to have reverted to self-governing towns, usually fortified places on hilltops. Continued contact with the Mediterranean, including with the **Greeks**, who had a brief presence on Spanish shores in the middle of the millennium, meant that these towns produced coins, texts and, particularly, fine sculpture, including such examples as the Dama de Baza, a lifesize seated goddess found in Granada province, and the Porcuna sculptures displayed in the provincial museum in Jaén.

As Phoenician power waned, their heirs and descendants, the **Carthaginians**, increased their operations in the western Mediterranean and settled throughout Andalucía, particularly at Cádiz. While the Phoenicians had enjoyed a mostly prosperous and peaceful relationship with the local peoples, the Carthaginians were more concerned with conquest and, under **Hamilcar Barca** and his relatives **Hasdrubal** and **Hannibal**, they took control of much of southern Spain and increased mining operations. The Iberian tribes, who included the **Turdetanians**, the group that had inherited the Tartessian mantle in the Guadalquivir basin, seem to have had mixed relations with the Barcid rulers. Some towns accepted Carthaginian control, while others resisted it.

Hispania

The Romans were bent on ending Punic power in the Mediterranean and soon realized that the peninsula was rapidly becoming a second Carthage. Roman troops arrived in Spain in 218 BC and Andalucía became one of the major theatres of the Second Punic War. Some of the local tribes, such as the Turdetanians, sided with the Romans against the Carthaginians and the final Roman victory came in

206 BC, at the Battle of Ilipa near Sevilla. The Carthaginians were kicked out of the peninsula.

During the war, the Romans had established the city of Itálica near Sevilla as a rest camp for dissatisfied Italian troops but it was only some time after the end of hostilities that the Romans appear to have developed an interest in the peninsula itself. Realizing the vast resources of the region, they set about conquering the whole of Hispania, a feat that they did not accomplish until late in the first century BC. It was the Romans that first created the idea of Spain as a single geographical entity, a concept it has struggled with ever since.

Rome initially divided the peninsula into two provinces, **Hispania Citerior** in the north and **Hispania Ulterior** in the south. Here, the military faced immediate problems from their one-time allies, the Turdetanians, who were not happy that the invaders hadn't returned home after defeating the Carthaginians. This rebellion was quelled brutally by Cato the Elder around 195 BC and, although there were several uprisings over the succeeding centuries, the Romans had far fewer problems in Andalucía than in the rest of the peninsula.

Part of this was due to the region's wealth. The ever-increasing mining operations mostly used slave labour and gave little back to the locals, but exports of olive oil, wine and *garum* meant the local economy thrived, despite the heavy tributes exacted by the Republic. Roman customs rubbed off on the Iberians and the local languages gradually disappeared as Latin became predominant.

The wealth of Hispania meant that it became an important pawn in the power struggles of the Roman republic and it was in Andalucía, near modern Bailén, that **Julius Caesar** finally defeated Pompey's forces in 45 BC. With peace established, Caesar set about establishing colonies in earnest; many of Andalucía's towns and cities were built or rebuilt by the Romans in this period. Julius knew the region pretty well; he had campaigned here in 68 BC and later had been governor of Hispania Ulterior. The contacts he had made during this period served him well and Caesar rewarded the towns that had helped him against Pompey, such as Sevilla and Cádiz, by conferring full Roman citizenship on the inhabitants. Later, Vespasian granted these rights to the whole of the peninsula.

Augustus redivided Hispania into three provinces; the southernmost, **Baetica**, roughly corresponded to modern Andalucía. Initially administered from Córdoba, the capital was switched to Hispalis (Sevilla), which, along with neighbouring Itálica, prospered under the Imperial regime. The south of Spain became a real Roman heartland, the most Roman of the Roman colonies. Itálica was the birthplace of the Emperor Trajan and sometime home of his protegé Hadrian, while the Seneca family originated in Córdoba. The first century AD was a time of much peace and prosperity and Andalucía's grandest Roman remains date largely from this period.

It was probably during this century that the bustling Andalucían ports heard their first whisperings of Christianity, which arrived early in the peninsula. Around this time, too, a Jewish population began to build up; the beginnings of what was a crucial segment of Andalucían society for 1500 years.

A gradual decline began late in the second century AD, with raids from North Africa nibbling at the edges of a weakening empire. The Iberian provinces took the wrong side in struggles for the emperorship and suffered as a result; by the fourth century, Cádiz was virtually in ruins and the lack of control meant that an almost feudal system developed, with wealthy citizens controlling local production from fortified villas. Christianity had become a dominant force, but religious squabblings exacerbated rather than eased the tension.

In the fifth century, as the Roman order tottered, various barbarian groups streamed across the Pyrenees and created havoc. **Alans** and **Vandals** established themselves in the south of Spain; it has been (almost certainly erroneously) suggested that the latter group lent their name to Andalucía. The Romans enlisted the Visigoths to restore order on their behalf. This they succeeded in doing, but they liked the look of the land and returned for good after they lost control of their French territories. After a period of much destruction and chaos, a fairly tenuous Visigothic control ensued. They used Sevilla as an early capital, but later transferred their seat of power to Toledo.

The Visigoths

While there is little enough archaeological and historical evidence from this period, what has been found shows that the Visigoths had inherited Roman customs and architecture to a large degree, while many finds exhibit highly sophisticated carving and metalworking techniques. The bishop and writer San Isidoro produced some of Europe's most important post-Roman texts from his base in Sevilla. There were likely comparatively few Visigoths; a small warrior class ruling with military strength best fits the evidence, and they seem to have fairly rapidly become absorbed into the local culture.

The politics of the Visigothic period are characterized by kinstrife and wranglings over Christian doctrine. Some of the numerous dynastic struggles were fought across a religious divide: the Visigothic monarchs were initially adherents of Arianism, a branch of Christianity that denied the coëval status of the Son in the Trinity. While the general population was Catholic, this wasn't necessarily a major stumbling block, but various pretenders to the throne used the theological question as a means for gaining support for a usurpment. During these struggles in the mid-sixth century, various of the pretenders called upon Byzantine support and Emperor Justinian I took advantage of the situation to annex the entire Andalucían coastline as a province, which was held for some 70 years. Inland Andalucía had proved difficult to keep in line for the Visigothic monarchs: King Agila was defeated by a rising in Córdoba and the Sevilla-based businessman Athanagild managed to maneouvre his way on to the throne. He and his successor Leovigild finally pacified the unruly Córdobans, but Leovigild faced a revolt in Andalucía from his own son, Hermenegild, who had converted to Catholicism. Father defeated offspring and the kingdom passed to Leovigild's younger son Reccared (AD 586-601), who wisely converted to Catholicism and established a period of relative peace and prosperity for the people of the peninsula.

San Isidoro

"No one can gain a full understanding of Spain without a knowledge of Saint Isidore" - Richard Ford

Born in AD 560, Isidoro succeeded his brother Leandro as Bishop of Sevilla. One of the most important intellectual figures of the Middle Ages, his prolific writings cover all subjects and were still popular at the time of the Renaissance. His *Etymologiae* was one of the first secular books in print when it appeared in AD 1472. The first encyclopedia written in the Christian west, it became the primary source for the 154 classical authors that Isidoro quoted. He also wrote on music, law, history and jurisprudence as well as doctrinal matters.

Isidoro is also recognized as an important church reformer and was responsible for the production of the so-called Mozarabic rite which is still practised in Toledo Cathedral today. His writings were an attempt to restore vigour and direction to a church that was in decline following the Visigothic invasions.

Another important element to Isidoro's writings were his prophecies, based both on the Bible and classical references. This element of his writings appealed to later generations living in the shadow of the Muslim conquests and was to be the source of many stories and legends. Following the expulsion of the Moors it seemed to some that an ancient prophecy was about to be fulfilled.

Isidoro died in Sevilla in AD 636 and his writings continued to inspire Spain for the next nine centuries. His body is now in León, moved there by Fernando I of Castilla who repatriated it to the Christian north around AD 1060.

The seventh century saw numerous changes of rulers, many of whom imposed increasingly severe strictures on the substantial Jewish population of the peninsula. Restrictions on owning property, attempted forced conversions and other impositions foreshadowed much later events in Spain. The Visigoths possibly paid a heavy price for this persecution; several historians opine that the Moorish invasion was substantially aided by the support of Jewish communities that (rightly, as it turned out) viewed the conquerors as liberators.

Al-Andalus

In AD 711 an event occurred that was to define Spanish history for the next eight centuries. The teachings of Mohammed had swept across North Africa and the Moors were to take most of Spain before the prophet had been dead for even a century. After a number of exploratory raids, Tarik, governor of Tanger, crossed the straits with a small force of mostly Berber soldiers. It is said that he named the large rock he found after himself; Jebel Tarik (the mountain of Tarik), a name which over time evolved into Gibraltar. Joined by a larger force under the command of the governor of North Africa, Musa ibn-Nusair, the Moors then defeated and slew the Visigothic king Roderic somewhere near Tarifa. The conquests continued under Musa's son Abd al-Aziz until almost the whole peninsula was in Moorish hands: the conquest had taken less than three years, an extraordinary feat. Soon the Muslim armies were well advanced on the *autoroutes* of southern France.

The Moors named their Iberian dominions Al-Andalus and while these lands grew and shrunk over time, the heartland was always in the south. After the conquest, Al-Andalus was administered by governors based in Córdoba, who ultimately answered to the Ummayad caliph in distant Damascus. This shift of the effective capital south from Toledo to Córdoba meant that the peninsula's focus was much more in Andalucía and, consequently, the Mediterranean and North Africa.

In AD 750, an event occurred in distant Damascus that was to shape the destiny of Moorish Spain. The Abbasid dynasty ousted the ruling Umayyad family and proceeded to massacre them. One prince, Abd al-Rahman, managed to escape the carnage and made his way to Spain in AD 756. Arriving in Córdoba, he contrived to gain and hold power in the city. Gradually taking control over more and more of Al-Andalus, he established the emirate of Córdoba, which was to rule the Moorish dominions in Spain for nearly three centuries.

Romantic depictions of Al-Andalus as a multicultural paradise are way off the mark; the situation is best described by Richard Fletcher as one of "grudging toleration, but toleration nonetheless". Christians and Jews were allowed relative freedom of worship and examples of persecution are comparatively few. Moorish texts throughout the history of Al-Andalus reveal a condescending attitude towards non-Muslims (and vice-versa in Christian parts of Spain), but it is probable that in day-to-day life there was large-scale cultural contact, a process described by Spanish historians as *convivencia* (cohabitation). The conversion of Christians and Jews to Islam was a gradual but constant process; this was no doubt given additional impetus by the fact that Muslims didn't pay any tax beyond the alms required as part of their faith. Christian converts to Islam were known as *muwallads*, while those who remained Christian under the rule of the Moors are called *mozárabes* or Mozarabs.

Arabic rapidly became the major language of southern Spain, even among non-Muslims. The number of Arabic words in modern Spanish attests to this. Many of them refer to agriculture and crops; the Moors brought with them vastly improved farming and irrigation methods, as well as a host of fruits and vegetables not grown before on the peninsula's soil. This, combined with wide and profitable trading routes in the Mediterranean, meant that Al-Andalus began to thrive economically, which must have assisted in the pacification of the region. Córdoba's Mezquita, begun in the eighth century, was expanded and made richer in various phases through this period; this can be seen as reflecting both the growing wealth and the increasing number of worshippers.

Geography divides Spain into distinct regions, which have tended to persist through time, and it was one of these – Asturias – that the Moors had trouble with. They were defeated in what was presumably a minor skirmish in AD 717 at Covadonga, in the far northern mountains. While the Moors weren't too rattled by this at the time, Spain views it today as a happening of immense significance, a victory against all odds and even a sort of mystical watershed where God proved himself to be on the Christian side. It was hardly a crippling blow to the Moors, but it probably sowed the seeds of what became the **Asturian** and **Leonese** monarchy. A curious development in many ways, this royal line emerged unconquered from the shadowy northern hills and forests. Whether they were a last bastion of Visigothic resistance, or whether they were just local folk ready to defend their lands, they established an organized little kingdom of sorts with a capital that shifted about but settled on Oviedo in AD 808.

The Asturian kingdom began to grow in strength and the long process of the *Reconquista*, the Christian reconquest of the peninsula, began. The northerners took advantage of cultural interchange with the south, which remained significant during the period despite the militarized zone in between, and were soon strong enough to begin pushing back. The loose Moorish authority in these lands certainly helped; the northern zone was more or less administered by warlords who were only partially controlled by the emirs and caliphs in Córdoba. Galicia and much of the north coast was reclaimed and in AD 914 the Asturian king Ordoño II reconquered León; the capital shortly moved to here and the line of kings took on the name of that town. As the Christians moved south, they re-settled many towns and villages that had lain in ruins since Roman times.

By the 10th century, the economy was booming in Córdoba and its dominions. A growing sophistication in politics and the arts was partly driven by cultured expats from Damascus and Baghdad who brought learning and fashions from the great cities of the Arab world. It was a time of achievement in literature, the sciences and engineering, including the works of classical writers such as Aristotle and Arabic treatises on subjects such as astronomy and engineering. The whole of Europe felt the benefit as knowledge permeated to the Christian north.

Little wonder then, that the emir Abd al-Rahman III (AD 912-961) felt in bullish mood. In AD 929 he gave himself the title of *caliph*, signalling a definitive break with the east as there can only be one caliph (ordained successor to Mohammed) and he was in Baghdad. Although he had no basis to name himself caliph, the declaration served to establish Al-Andalus as a free-standing Islamic kingdom in the west. Córdoba at this time probably had over 100,000 inhabitants, which would have put it at the same level as Constantinople and far above any other European city. Abd al-Rahman celebrated the new status by building an incredibly lavish palace and administration complex, **Madinat al-Zahra (Medina Azahara)**, to the west of the city.

But Asturias/León wasn't the only Christian power to have developed. The Basques had been quietly pushing outwards too and their small mountain

BACKGROUND

The Conqueror

Mohammed ibn-Abi al Ma'afari was born to a poor family near Algeciras around AD 938. Known to latter generations as Al-Manzur or 'the conqueror', he is one of the most remarkable figures of the Middle Ages, representing both the strength of Muslim Spain and its ultimate failure. A lawyer, he succeeded in reforming the administration of the Caliphate and in modernizing its army before getting his chance at power as one of three co-regents named to govern while the child-caliph Hisham II grew to maturity. Al-Manzur managed to manoeuvre the other co-regents out of the way, having one imprisoned and murdered and engaging the forces of the other in battle. Meanwhile, he beguiled Hisham with wine, women, and song so successfully that once the caliph grew up he never made a political decision, letting Al-Manzur rule in his stead. The regent was so sure of his position that he even took the title of king in AD 996.

While regent, he launched a series of lightning raids across the Christian north. His army, made up of mercenary Slavs, Christian renegades and North African Berbers, sacked Zamora and Simancas in AD 981, Barcelona in AD 985 and León in AD 987. The Leonese king Bermudo had broken an agreement to pay tribute and was forced to flee to the Asturian mountains. In AD 997 he embarked on his final campaign to extinguish Christian opposition. He took A Coruña and the holy city of Santiago where he removed the bells of the cathedral to the mosque of Córdoba. On encountering a lone priest protecting the shrine of St James he is said to have ordered his men to leave the holy relics of the city untouched.

While his military exploits were undoubtedly one of the period's great feats of generalship, Al-Manzur was not really a bloodthirsty tyrant. Under his guidance a university was established in Córdoba and he was a great patron of the arts and science. On his many military campaigns both in Spain and North Africa he took a library of books. It was under Al-Manzur that the final expansion of the Mezquita took place.

After an inconclusive battle in 1002 at Calatañazor in Castilla, Al-Manzur died of natural causes. The relief of the Christians was immense, even more so when the caliphate, without the Conqueror at the helm, disintegrated six years later.

kingdom of Navarra grew rapidly. Aragón emerged and gained power and size via a dynastic union with Catalunya. The entity that came to dominate Spain, Castilla, was born at this time too. In the middle of the 10th century, a Burgos noble, Fernán González, declared independence from the kingdom of León and began to rally disparate Christian groups in the region. He was so successful in this endeavour that it wasn't long before his successors labelled themselves kings.

Both the Christian and Muslim powers were painfully aware of their vulnerability and constructed a series of massive fortresses that faced each other across the central plains. The Muslim fortresses were particularly formidable; high eyries with commanding positions, accurately named the 'front teeth' of Al-Andalus. Relations between Christian and Muslim Spain were curious. While there were frequent campaigns, raids and battles, there was also a high level of peaceful contact and diplomacy. Even the fighting was far from being a confrontation of implacably opposed rivals: Christian knights and Moorish mercenaries hired themselves out to either side, none more so than the famous El Cid.

The caliphate faced a very real threat from the Fatimid dynasty in North Africa and campaigning in the Christian north was one way to fund the fortification of the Mediterranean coast. No-one campaigned more successfully than the formidable Al-Manzur (see box, opposite), who, while regent for the child-caliph Hisham II, conducted no fewer than 57 victorious sallies into the peninsula, succeeding in sacking almost every city in Northern Spain in a 30-year campaign of terror. Al-Manzur was succeeded by his equally adept son Abd al-Malik, but when he died young in 1008, the caliphate disintegrated with two rival Ummayad claimants seeking to fill the power vacuum.

Twenty years of civil war followed and Córdoba was more or less destroyed. Both sides employed a variety of Christian and Muslim mercenaries to prosecute their claims to the caliphal throne; the situation was bloody and chaotic in the extreme. When the latest puppet caliph was deposed in 1031, any pretence of centralized government evaporated and Berber generals, regional administrators and local opportunists seized power in towns across Al-Andalus, forming the small city-states known as the *taifa* kingdoms; *taifa* means faction in Arabic.

This first *taifa* period lasted for most of the rest of the 11th century and in many ways sounded an early death-knell for Muslim Spain. Petty rivalries between the neighbouring *taifas* led to recruitment of Christian military aid in exchange for large sums of cash. This influx led in turn to the strengthening of the northern kingdoms and many *taifas* were then forced to pay tribute, or protection money, to Christian rulers or face obliteration.

The major *taifas* in Andalucía were Sevilla and Granada, which gradually swallowed up several of their smaller neighbours. The Abbadid rulers of Sevilla led a hedonistic life, the kings Al-Mu'tadid and his son Al-Mu'tamid penning poetry between revelries and romantic liaisons. A pogrom against the Jewish population in 1066 indicated that there was little urban contentment behind the luxuriant façade.

The Christian north lost little time in taking advantage of the weak *taifa* states. As well as exacting punitive tribute, the Castilian king Alfonso VI had his eye on conquests and crossed far beyond the former frontline of the Duero valley. His capture of highly symbolic Toledo, the old Visigothic capital and Christian centre, in 1085, finally set alarm bells ringing in the verse-addled brains of the *taifa* kings.

They realized they needed help, and they called for it across the Straits to Morocco. Since the middle of the 11th century, a group of tribesmen known as the **Almoravids** had been establishing control there and their leader, Yusuf, was invited across to Al-Andalus to help combat Alfonso VI. A more unlikely alliance is hard to imagine; the Almoravids were barely-literate desert warriors with a strong and fundamentalist Islamic faith, a complete contrast to the *taifa* rulers in their blossom-scented pleasure domes. The Almoravid armies defeated Alfonso near Badajoz in 1086 but were appalled at the state of Islam in Al-Andalus, so Yusuf decided to stay and establish a stricter observance. He rapidly destroyed the *taifa* system and established governors, answerable to Marrakech, in the major towns, including Sevilla, having whisked the poet-king off to wistful confinement in Fez.

Almoravid rule was marked by a more aggressive approach to the Christian north, which was matched by the other side. Any hope of retaking much territory soon subsided, as rebellions from the local Andalusi and pressure from another dynasty, the Almohads in Morocco, soon took their toll. This was compounded by another factor: tempted no doubt by big lunches, tapas, siestas and free-poured spirits, the hardline Almoravids were lapsing into softer ways. Control again dissolved into local *taifas*; Alfonso VII took advantage, seizing Córdoba in 1146 and Almería in 1147.

They weren't held for long, though. The Almohads, who by now controlled Morocco, began crossing the Straits to intervene in Andalusi military affairs. Although similarly named and equally hard line in their Islamism, the Almohads were significantly different to the Almoravids, with a canny grasp of politics and advanced military tactics. They founded the settlement of Gibraltar in 1159, took back Almería and Córdoba and gained control over the whole of what is now Andalucía by about 1172. Much surviving military architecture in Andalucía was built by the Almohads, including the great walls and towers of Sevilla. Yet they too lapsed into decadence, and bungled planning led to the very costly military defeat at Las Navas de Tolosa at the hands of Alfonso VIII in 1212. This was a major blow. Alfonso's son Fernando III (1217-1252) capitalized on his father's success, taking Córdoba in 1236, Jaén, the 'Iron Gate' of Andalucía, in 1246, and then Sevilla, the Almohad capital, in 1248, after a two-year siege. The loss of the most important city of Al-Andalus, mourned across the whole Muslim world, was effectively the end of Moorish power in Spain, although the emirate of Granada lingered on for another 250 years. Fernando, sainted for his efforts, kicked out all Sevilla's Moorish inhabitants, setting a pattern of intolerance towards the *mudéjares*, as those Muslims who lived under Christian rule came to be called.

What was left of Muslim Spain was the emirate of Granada. The nobleman Mohammed Ibn-Yusuf Ibn-Nasr set himself up here as ruler in 1237 and gave his name to the Nasrid dynasty. Although nominally independent, it was to a large extent merely a vassal of the Castilian kings. Mohammed surrendered Jaén and began paying tribute to Fernando III in exchange for not being attacked in Granada. He even sent a detachment of troops to help besiege Sevilla, a humiliation that eloquently shows how little real power he had. His territory included a long stretch of the Andalucían coastline from the Atlantic eastwards past Almería and a small inland area that included Granada itself, Antequera and Ronda.

Meanwhile, the Christians were consolidating their hold on most of Andalucía, building churches and cathedrals over the mosques they found and trying to find settlers to work the vast new lands at their disposal as many of the Moors had fled to the kingdom of Granada or across the sea to North Africa. Nobles involved in the *Reconquista* claimed vast tracts of territory; estates known as *latifundias* that still exist today and that have been the cause of numerous social problems in Andalucía over the centuries.

The Christians still had some fighting to do. The Marinid rulers of Morocco were a constant menace and managed to take Algeciras in the late 13th century. Tarifa was recaptured in 1292 and became the scene of the famous heroic actions of Guzmán 'El Bueno' who defended it against another siege two years later. There were regular, if half-hearted, Christian campaigns agaist Nasrid Granada, one of which involved Sir James 'the Black' Douglas, who met his death carrying the embalmed heart of Robert the Bruce into combat at Teba in 1329.

The Nasrid kingdom continued to survive, partly because its boundaries were extremely well fortified with a series of thousands of defensive towers. The Alhambra as we know it was mostly built under Mohammad V in the second half of the 14th century; at the same time, the enlightened Castilian king Pedro I was employing Moorish craftsmen to recreate Sevilla's Alcázar in sumptuous style.

The Golden Age

In the 15th century, there were regular rebellions and much kinstrife over succession in the Nasrid kingdom, which was beginning to seem ripe for the plucking. One of the reasons this hadn't yet happened was that the Christian kingdoms were involved in similar succession disputes. Then, in 1469, an event occurred that was to spell the end for the Moorish kingdom and have a massive impact on the history of the world. The heir to the Aragonese throne, Fernando, married Isabel, heiress of Castilla, in a secret ceremony in Valladolid. The implications were enormous. Aragón was still a power in the Mediterranean (Fernando was also king of Sicily) and Castilla's domain covered much of the peninsula. The unification under the *Reyes Católicos*, as the monarchs became known, marked the beginnings of Spain as we know it today. Things didn't go smoothly at first, however. There were plenty of opponents to the union and forces in support of Juana, Isabel's elder (but claimed by her to be illegitimate) sister waged wars across Castilla.

When the north was once more at peace, the monarchs found that they ruled the entire peninsula except for Portugal, with which a peace had just been negotiated, the small mountain kingdom of Navarra, which Fernando stood a decent chance of inheriting at some stage anyway, and the decidedly un-Catholic Nasrids in their sumptuous southern palaces. The writing was on the wall and Fernando and Isabel began their campaign. Taking Málaga in 1487 and Almería in 1490, they were soon at Granada's gates. The end came with a whimper, as the vacillating King Boabdil, who had briefly allied himself with the monarchs in a struggle against his father, elected not to go down fighting and surrendered the keys of the great city on New Year's Day in 1492 in exchange for a small principality in the Alpujarra region (which in the end he decided not to take and left for Morocco). His mother had little sympathy as he looked back longingly at the city he had left. "You weep like a woman," she allegedly scolded, "for what you could not defend like a man".

The Catholic Monarchs had put an end to Al-Andalus, which had endured in various forms for the best part of 800 years. They celebrated in true Christian style by kicking the Jews out of Spain. Andalucía's Jewish population had been hugely significant for a millennium and a half, heavily involved in commerce, shipping and literature throughout the peninsula. But hatred of them had begun to grow in the 14th century and there had been many pogroms, including an especially vicious one in 1391, which began in Sevilla and spread to most other cities in Christian Spain. Many converted during these years to escape the murderous atmosphere; they became known as *conversos*. The decision to expel those who hadn't converted was far more that of the pious Isabel than the pragmatic Fernando and has to be seen in the light of the paranoid Christianizing climate. The Jews were given four months to leave the kingdom and even the *conversos* soon found themselves under the iron hammer of the Inquisition.

The valleys of the Alpujarra region south of Granada were where many refugees from previously conquered Moorish areas had fled to from the Christians. When Granada itself fell, many Muslims came here to settle on the rich agricultural land. Although under the dominion of the Catholic Monarchs, it was still largely Muslim in character and it is no surprise that, as new anti-Islamic legislation began to bite, it was here that rebellion broke out. From 1499, the inhabitants fought the superior Christian armies for over two years until the revolt was bloodily put down. In no mood for conciliation, Fernando and Isabel gave the Moors the choice of baptism (converts became known as *moriscos*) or expulsion. Emigration wasn't feasible for most; a vast sum of money had to be handed over for the 'privilege' and in most cases parents weren't allowed to take their children with them.

There was another *morisco* revolt in 1568, again centred on the Alpujarra region. After this, there was forcible dispersal and resettlement of their population throughout Spain. Finally, the *moriscos* too were expelled (in 1609) by Felipe III. It is thought that the country lost some 300,000 of its population and parts of Spain have perhaps still not wholly recovered from this self-inflicted purge of the majority of its intellectual, commercial and professional talent. The lack of cultural diversity led to long-term stagnation. The ridiculous doctrine of *limpieza de sangre* (purity of blood) became all-important; the enduring popularity of pig meat surely owes something to these days, when openly eating these foods proved that one wasn't Muslim or Jewish.

But we move back for a moment to 1492. One of the crowd watching Boabdil hand the keys to Granada over to Fernando and Isabel was Cristóbal Colón (Christopher Columbus), who had been petitioning the royal couple for ships and funds to mount an expedition to sail westwards to the Indies. Finally granted his request, he set off from Palos de la Frontera near Huelva and, after a deal of hardship, reached what he thought was his goal. In the wake of Columbus's discovery, the treaty of Tordesillas in 1494 partitioned the Atlantic between Spain and Portugal and led to the era of Spanish colonization of the Americas. In many ways, this was an extension of the *Reconquista* as young men hardened on the Castilian and Extremaduran *meseta* crossed the seas with zeal for conquest, riches and land. Andalucía was both enriched and crippled by this exodus: while the cities flourished on the New World booty and trade, the countryside was denuded of people to work the land. The biggest winner proved to be Sevilla, which was granted a monopoly over New World trade by the Catholic Monarchs in 1503. It grew rapidly and became one of Western Europe's foremost cities. In 1519 another notable endeavour began here. Ferdinand Magellan set sail from Triana, via Sanlúcar de Barrameda, in an attempt to circumnavigate the world. He didn't make it, dying halfway, but one of the expedition's ships did. Skippered by a Basque, Juan Sebastián Elkano, it arrived some three years later.

Isabel died in 1504, but refused to settle her Castilian throne on her husband, Fernando, to his understandable annoyance, as the two had succeeded in uniting virtually the whole of modern Spain under their joint rule. The inheritance passed to their mad daughter, Juana la Loca, and her husband, Felipe of Burgundy (el Hermoso or the Fair), who came to Spain in 1506 to claim their inheritance. Felipe soon died, however, and his wife's obvious inability to govern led to Fernando being recalled as regent of the united Spain until the couple's son, Carlos, came of age. During this period Fernando completed the boundaries of modern Spain by annexing Navarra. On his deathbed he reluctantly agreed to name Carlos heir to Aragón and its territories, thus preserving the unity he and Isabel had forged. Carlos I of Spain (Carlos V) inherited vast tracts of European land; Spain and southern Italy from his maternal grandparents, and Austria, Burgundy and the Low Countries from his paternal ones. He was shortly named Holy Roman Emperor and if all that worldly power weren't enough, his friend, aide and tutor, Adrian of Utrecht, was soon elected Pope.

The first two Habsburg monarchs, Carlos V and then his son Felipe II relied on the income from the colonies to pursue wars (often unwillingly) on several European fronts. It couldn't last; Spain's Golden Age has been likened by historian Felipe Fernández-Armesto to a dog walking on its hind legs. While Sevilla prospered from the American expansion, the provinces declined, hastened by a drain of citizens to the New World. The *comunero* revolt expressed the frustrations of a region that was once the focus of optimistic Christian conquest and agricultural wealth, but had now become peripheral to the designs of a 'foreign' monarchy. Resentment was exacerbated by the fact that the king still found it difficult to extract taxes from the *cortes* of Aragón or Catalunya, so Castilla (of which Andalucía was a part) bankrolled a disproportionate amount of the crippling costs of the running of a worldwide empire. The growing administrative requirements of managing an empire had forced the previously itinerant Castilian monarchs to choose a capital and Felipe II picked the small town of Madrid in 1561, something of a surprise, as Sevilla or Valladolid were more obvious choices. Although central, Madrid was remote, tucked away behind a shield of hills in the interior. This seemed in keeping with the somewhat paranoid nature of Habsburg rule. And beyond all other things, they were paranoid about threats to the Catholic religion; the biggest of which, of course, they perceived to be Protestantism. This paranoia was costly in the extreme.

The struggle of the Spanish monarchy to control the spread of Protestantism was a major factor in the decline of the empire. Felipe II fought expensive and ultimately unwinnable wars in Flanders that bankrupted the state; while within the country the absolute ban on the works of heretical philosophers, scientists and theologists left Spain behind in Renaissance Europe. In the 18th century, for example, the so-called Age of Enlightenment in Western Europe, theologists at the noble old university of Salamanca debated what language the angels spoke; that Castilian was proposed as a likely answer is certain. Felipe II's successors didn't have his strength of character; Felipe III was ineffectual and dominated by his advisors, while Felipe IV, so sensitively portrayed by Velázquez, tried hard but was indecisive and unfortunate, despite the best efforts of his favourite, the remarkable Conde-Duque de Olivares. As well as being unwillingly involved in several costly wars overseas, there was also a major rebellion in Catalunya in the mid-17th century. The decline of the monarchy parallelled a physical decline in the monarchs, as the inbred Habsburgs became more and more deformed and weak; the last of them, Carlos II, was a tragic victim of contorted genetics who died childless and plunged the nation into a war of succession. "Castilla has made Spain and Castilla has destroyed it," commented early 20th century essayist José Ortega y Gasset. While the early 17th century saw the zenith of the Seville school of painting, the city was in decline; the expulsion of the *moriscos* had removed a vital labour force and merchants and bankers were packing up and going elsewhere as the crown's economic problems led to increasingly punitive taxation. The century saw several plagues in Andalucían cities and Sevilla lost an incredible half of its inhabitants in 1649.

The death of poor heirless Carlos II was a long time coming and foreign powers were circling to try and secure a favourable succession to the throne of Spain. Carlos eventually named the French duke Felipe de Bourbon as his successor, much to the concern of England and Holland, who declared war on France. War broke out throughout Spain until the conflict's eventual resolution at the Treaty of Utrecht; at which Britain received Gibraltar, and Spain also lost its Italian and Low Country possessions.

The Bourbon dynasty succeeded in bringing back a measure of stability and wealth to Spain in the 18th century. Sevilla's decline and the silting up of the Guadalquivir led to the monarchs establishing Cádiz as the centre for New World trade in its place and Spain's oldest city prospered again. The Catholic church, however, was in a poor state intellectually and came to rely more and more on cults and fiestas to keep up the interest of the populace: many of Andalucía's colourful religious celebrations were formed during this period. The 18th century also saw the energetic reformer Pedro de Olavide, chief adviser to King Carlos III, try to repopulate rural Andalucía by creating planned towns and encouraging foreign settlers to live in them.

The 19th century in Andalucía and Spain was turbulent to say the least. The 18th century had ended with a Spanish-French conflict in the wake of the French revolution. Peace was made after two years, but worse was to follow. First was a heavy defeat for a joint Spanish-French navy by Nelson off Cabo Trafalgar near Cádiz. Next Napoleon tricked Carlos IV. Partitioning Portugal between France and Spain seemed like a good idea to Spain, which had always coveted its western neighbour. It wasn't until the French armies seemed more interested in Madrid than Lisbon that Carlos IV got the message. Forced to abdicate in favour of his rebellious son Fernando, he was then summoned to a conference with Bonaparte at Bayonne, with his son, wife and Manuel Godoy, his able and trusted adviser (who is often said to have been loved even more by the queen than the king). Napoleon had his own brother Joseph (known among Spaniards as *Pepe Botellas* for his heavy drinking) installed on the throne.

On 2 May 1808 (still a red-letter day in Spain), the people revolted against this arrogant gesture and Napoleon sent in the troops later that year. Soon after, a hastily assembled Spanish army inflicted a stunning defeat on the French at Bailén, near Jaén; the Spaniards were then joined by British and Portuguese forces and the ensuing few years are known in Spain as the Guerra de Independencia (War of Independence). The allied forces under Wellington won important battles after the initiative had been taken by the French. The behaviour of both sides was brutal both on and off the battlefield. Marshal Soult's long retreat across the region saw him loot town after town; his men robbed tombs and burned priceless archives. The allied forces were little better; the men Wellington had referred to as the 'scum of the earth' sacked the towns they conquered with similar destructiveness.

Significant numbers of Spaniards had been in favour of the French invasion and were opposed to the liberal republican movements that sprang up in its wake. In 1812, a revolutionary council in Cádiz, on the point of falling to the French, drafted a constitution proclaiming a democratic parliamentary monarchy of sorts. Liberals had high hopes that this would be brought into effect at the end of the war, but the returning king, Fernando, revoked it. Meanwhile, Spain was on the point of losing its South American colonies, which were being mobilized under *libertadores* such as Simón Bolívar. Spain sent troops to restore control; a thankless assignment for the soldiers involved. One of the armies was preparing to leave Cádiz in 1820 when the commander, Rafael de Riego, invoked the 1812 constitution and refused to fight under the 'unconstitutional' monarchy. Much of the army joined him and the king was forced to recognize the legality of the constitution. Things soon dissolved though, with the 'liberals' (the first use of the word) being split into factions and opposed by the church and aristocracy. Eventually, king Fernando called on the king of France to send an invading army; the liberals were driven backwards to Sevilla, then to Cádiz, where they were defeated and Riego taken to his execution in Madrid. In many ways this conflict mirrored the later Spanish Civil War. Riego, who remained (and remains) a hero of the democratically minded, did not die in vain; his stand impelled much of Europe on the road to constitutional democracy, although it took Spain itself over a century and a half to find democratic stability.

The remainder of the century was to see clash after clash of liberals against conservatives, progressive cities against reactionary countryside, restrictive centre against outward-looking periphery. Spain finally lost its empire, as the strife-torn homeland could do little against the independence movements of Latin America.

When Fernando died, another war of succession broke out, this time between supporters of his brother Don Carlos and his infant daughter Isabella. The so-called Carlist Wars of 1833-1839, 1847-1849 (although this is sometimes not counted as one) and 1872-1876 were politically complex. Don Carlos represented conservatism and his support was drawn from a number of sources. Wealthy landowners, the church and the reactionary peasantry, with significant French support, lined up against the loyalist army, the liberals and the urban middle and working classes. In between and during the wars, a series of *pronunciamientos* (coups d'état) plagued the monarchy. In 1834, after Fernando's death, another, far less liberal constitution was drawn up. An important development for Andalucía took place in 1835 when the Prime Minister, desperate for funds to prosecute the war against the Carlists, confiscated church and monastery property in the Disentailment Act. The resulting sale of the vast estates aided nobody but the large landowners, who bought them up at bargain prices, further skewing the distribution of arable land in Andalucía towards the wealthy.

Despite the grinding poverty, the middle years of the 19th century saw the beginnings of what was eventually to save Andalucía: tourism. Travellers, such as Washington Irving, Richard Ford and Prosper Merimée, came to the region and enthralled the world with tales of sighing Moorish princesses, feisty *sevillanas*, bullfights, gypsies, bandits and passion. While to the 21st-century eye, the uncritical romanticism of these accounts is evident, they captured much of the magic that contemporary visitors still find in the region and have inspired generations of travellers to investigate Spain's south.

During the third Carlist war, the king abdicated and the short-lived First Spanish Republic was proclaimed, ended by a military-led restoration a year later. The Carlists were defeated but remained strong and played a prominent part in the Spanish Civil War. (Indeed, there's still a Carlist party.) As if generations of war weren't enough, the wine industry of Andalucía received a crippling blow with the arrival of the phylloxera pest, which devastated the region.

The 1876 constitution proclaimed by the restored monarchy after the third Carlist war provided for a peaceful alternation of power between liberal and conservative parties. In the wake of decades of strikes and *pronunciamientos* this was not a bad solution and the introduction of the vote for the whole male population in 1892 offered much hope. The ongoing curse, however, was *caciquismo*, a system whereby elections and governments were hopelessly rigged by influential local groups of 'mates'.

Spain lost its last overseas possessions; Cuba, Puerto Rico and the Phillippines, in the 'Disaster' of 1898. The introspective turmoil caused by this event gave the name to the '1898 generation', a forward-thinking movement of artists, philosophers and poets among whom were numbered the poets Antonio Machado and Juan Ramón Jiménez, the philosophers José Ortega y Gasset and Miguel de Unamuno and the painter Ignacio de Zuloaga. It was a time of discontent, with regular strikes culminating in the Semana Trágica (tragic week) in Barcelona in 1909, a week of church-burning and rioting sparked by the government's decision to send a regiment of Catalan conscripts to fight in the 'dirty war' in Morocco; the revolt was then brutally suppressed by the army. The growing disaffectation of farmworkers in Andalucía, forced for centuries into seasonal labour on the vast *latifundias* with no security and minimal earnings, led to a strong anarchist movement in the region. The CNT, the most prominent of the 20th-century anarchist confederations, was founded in Sevilla in 1910.

The Second Republic

The early years of the 20th century saw repeated changes of government under King Alfonso XIII. A massive defeat in Morocco in 1921 increased the discontent with the monarch, but General Miguel Primo de Rivera, a native of Jerez de la Frontera, led a coup and installed himself as dictator under Alfonso in 1923. One of his projects was the grandiose Ibero-American exhibition in Sevilla. The preparation for this lavish event effectively created the modern city we know today and, despite bankrupting the city, set the framework for a 20th-century urban centre.

Primo de Rivera's rule was relatively benign, but growing discontent eventually forced the king to dismiss him. Having broken his coronation oath to uphold the constitution, Alfonso himself was soon toppled as republicanism swept the country. The anti-royalists achieved excellent results in elections in 1931 and the king drove to Cartagena and took a boat out of the country to exile. The Second Republic was joyfully proclaimed by the left.

Things moved quickly in the short period of the republic. The new leftist government moved fast to drastically reduce the church's power. The haste was ill-advised and triumphalist and served to severely antagonize the conservatives and the military. The granting of home rule to Catalunya was even more of a blow to the establishment and their belief in Spain as an indissoluble *patria*, or fatherland.

Through this period, there was increasing anarchist activity in Andalucía, where land was seized as a reaction to the archaic *latifundia* system under which prospects for the workers, who were virtually serfs, were nil. Anarchist cooperatives were formed to share labour and produce in many of the region's rural areas. Squabbling among leftist factions contributed to the government's lack of control of the country, which propelled the right to substantial gains in elections in 1933. Government was eventually formed by a centrist coalition, with the right powerful enough to heavily influence lawmaking. The 1933 elections also saw José Antonio Primo de Rivera, son of the old dictator, elected to a seat on a fascist platform. Although an idealist and no man of violence, he founded the Falange, a group of fascist youth that became an increasingly powerful force and one which was responsible for some of the most brutal deeds before, during and immediately after the Spanish Civil War.

The new government set about reversing the reforms of its predecessors; provocative and illegal infractions of labour laws by employers didn't help the workers' moods. Independence rumblings in Catalunya and the Basque country began to gather momentum, but it was in Asturias that the major confrontation took place. The left, mainly consisting of armed miners, seized the civil buildings of the province and the government response was harsh, with generals Goded and Franco embarking on a brutal spree of retribution with their well-trained Moroccan troops.

The left was outraged and the right feared complete revolution; the centre ceased to exist, as citizens and politicians were forced to one side or the other. The elections of February 1936 were very close, but the left unexpectedly defeated the right. In an increasingly violent climate, mobilized Socialist youth and the Falange were clashing daily, while land seizures continued. A group of generals began to plan a coup and in July 1936 a military conspiracy saw garrisons throughout Spain rise against the government and try to seize control of their provinces and towns. Within a few days, battle lines were clearly drawn between the Republicans (government) and the Nationalists, a coalition of military, Carlists, fascists and the Christian right. Most of northern Spain rapidly went under Nationalist control, while Madrid remained Republican. In Andalucía, Córdoba, Cádiz, Sevilla, Huelva and Granada were taken by Nationalists, but the remainder was in loyalist hands.

In the immediate aftermath of the uprising, frightening numbers of civilians were shot behind the lines, including the Granadan poet, Federico García Lorca. This brutality continued throughout the war, with chilling atrocities committed on both sides.

The most crucial blow of the war was struck early. Francisco Franco, one of the army's best generals, had been posted to the Canary Islands by the government, who were rightly fearful of coup attempts. As the uprising occurred, Franco was flown to Morocco where he took command of the crack North African legions. The difficulty was crossing into Spain: this was achieved in August in an airlift across the Straits of Gibraltar by German planes. Franco swiftly advanced through Andalucía where his battle-hardened troops met with little resistance. Meanwhile, the other main battle lines were north of Madrid and in Aragón, where the Republicans made a determined early push for Zaragoza.

At a meeting of the revolutionary generals in October 1936, Franco had himself declared *generalísimo*, the supreme commander of the Nationalists. Few could have suspected that he would rule the nation for nearly four decades. Although he had conquered swathes of Andalucía and Extremadura with little difficulty, the war wasn't to be as short as it might have appeared. Advancing on Madrid, he detoured to relieve the besieged garrison at Toledo; by the time he turned his attention back to the capital, the defences had been shored up and Madrid resisted throughout the war.

A key aspect of the Spanish Civil War was international involvement. Fascist Germany and Italy had troops to test, and a range of weaponry to play with; these countries gave massive aid to the Nationalist cause as a rehearsal for the Second World War, which was appearing increasingly inevitable. Russia provided the Republicans with some material, but inscrutable Stalin never committed his full support. Other countries, such as Britain, USA and France, disgracefully maintained a charade of international non-intervention despite the flagrant breaches by the above nations. Notwithstanding, thousands of volunteers mobilized to form the international brigades to help out the Republicans. Enlisting for idealistic reasons to combat the rise of fascism, many of these soldiers were writers and poets such as George Orwell and WH Auden.

Although Republican territory was split geographically, far more damage was done to their cause by ongoing and bitter infighting between anarchists, socialists, Soviet-backed communists and independent communists. There was constant struggling for power, political manoeuvring, backstabbing and outright violence, which the well-organized Nationalists must have watched with glee. The climax came in Barcelona in May 1937, when the Communist party took up arms against the anarchists and the POUM, an independent communist group. The city declined into a mini civil war of its own until order was restored. Morale, however, had taken a fatal blow.

Cities continued to fall to the Nationalists, for whom the German Condor legion proved a decisive force. In the south, the armies were under the command of Gonzalo Queipo de Llano, who though of broadly republican sympathies, was one of the original conspirators, and had expertly taken Sevilla at the beginning of things. Although his propaganda broadcasts throughout the war revealed him to be a kind of psychopathic humourist, this charismatic aristocrat was an impressive general and took Málaga in early 1937. Fleeing refugees were massacred by tanks and aircraft. Republican hopes now rested solely in the outbreak of a Europe-wide war. Franco had set up base appropriately in deeply conservative Burgos; Nationalist territory was the venue for many brutal reprisals against civilians perceived as leftist, unionist, democratic, or owning a tasty little piece of land on the edge of the village. Republican atrocities in many areas were equally appalling although rarely sanctioned or perpetrated by the government.

The Republicans made a couple of last-ditch efforts in early 1938 at Teruel and in the Ebro valley but were beaten in some of the most gruelling fighting of the Civil War. The Nationalists reached the Mediterranean, dividing Catalunya from the rest of Republican territory and, after the ill-fated Republican offensive over the Ebro, putting Barcelona under intense pressure; it finally fell in January 1939. Even at this late stage, given united resistance, the Republicans could have held out a while longer and the World War might have prevented a Franco victory, but it wasn't to be. The fighting spirit had largely dissipated and the infighting led to meek capitulation. Franco entered Madrid and the war was declared over on 1 April 1939.

If Republicans were hoping that this would signal the end of the slaughter and bloodshed, they didn't know the *generalísimo* well enough. A vengeful spate of executions, lynchings, imprisonments and torture ensued and the dull weight of the new regime stifled growth and optimism. Although many thousands of Spaniards fought in the Second World War (on both sides), Spain remained nominally neutral. After meeting Franco at Hendaye, Hitler declared that he would prefer to have three or four teeth removed than have to do so again. Franco had his eye on French Morocco and was hoping to be granted it for minimal Spanish involvement; Hitler accurately realized that the country had little more to give in the way of war effort and didn't offer an alliance.

The post-war years were tough in Spain, particularly in poverty-stricken Andalucía, where the old system was back in place and the workers penniless. Franco was an international outcast and the 1940s and 1950s were bleak times. Thousands of Andalucíans left in search of employment and a better life in Europe, the USA and Latin America. The Cold War was to prove Spain's saviour. Franco was nothing if not anti-communist and the USA began to see his potential as an ally.

Eisenhower offered to provide a massive aid package in exchange for Spanish support against the Eastern Bloc. In practice, this meant the creation of American airbases on Spanish soil; one of the biggest is at Rota, just outside Cádiz.

The dollars were dirty, but the country made the most of them; Spain boomed in the 1960s as industry finally took off and the flood of tourism to the Andalucían coasts began in earnest. But dictatorship was no longer fashionable in western Europe and Spain was regarded as a slightly embarassing cousin. It was not invited to join the European Economic Community (EEC) and it seemed as if nothing was going to really change until Franco died. He finally did, in 1975, and his appointed successor, King Juan Carlos I, the grandson of Alfonso XIII, took the throne of a country burning with democratic desires.

La Transición

The king was initially predicted to be just a pet of Franco's and therefore committed to maintaining the stultifying status quo, but he surprised everyone by acting swiftly to appoint the young Adolfo Suárez as prime minister. Suárez bullied the parliament into approving a new parliamentary system; political parties were legalized in 1977 and elections held in June that year. The return to democracy was known as *la transición*; the accompanying cultural explosion became known as *la movida (madrileña)*. Suárez's centrist party triumphed and he continued his reforms. The 1978 constitution declared Spain a parliamentary monarchy with no official religion; Franco must have turned in his grave and Suárez faced increasing opposition from the conservative elements in his own party. He resigned in 1981 and as his successor was preparing to take power, the good old Spanish tradition of the *pronunciamiento* came to the fore once again. A detachment of *Guardia Civil* stormed parliament in their comedy hats and Lieutenant Colonel Tejero, pistol waving and moustache twitching, demanded everyone hit the floor. After a tense few hours in which it seemed that the army might come out in support of Tejero, the king remained calm and, dressed in his capacity as head of the armed forces, assured the people of his commitment to democracy. The coup attempt thus failed and Juan Carlos was seen in an even better light.

In 1982, the Socialist government (PSOE) of Felipe González was elected. Hailing from Sevilla, he was committed to improving conditions and infrastructure in his native Andalucía. The single most important legislation since the return to democracy was the creation of the *comunidades autónomas*, in which the regions of Spain were given their own parliaments, which operate with varying degrees of freedom from the central government. This came to bear in 1983, although it was a process initiated by Suárez. Sevilla became the capital of the Andalucían region.

The Socialists held power for 14 years and oversaw Spain's entry into the EEC (now EU) in 1986, from which it has benefited immeasurably, although rural Andalucía remains poor by western European standards. But mutterings of several scandals began to plague the PSOE government and González was really disgraced when he was implicated in having commissioned death squads with the aim of terrorizing the Basques into renouncing terrorism, which few of them supported in any case.

Culture

Architecture

Spain's architectural heritage is one of Europe's richest and certainly its most diverse, due in large part to the dual influences of European Christian and Islamic styles during the eight centuries of Moorish presence in the peninsula. Another factor is economic: both during the *Reconquista* and in the wake of the discovery of the Americas, money seemed limitless and vast building projects were undertaken. Entire treasure fleets were spent in erecting lavish churches and monasteries on previously Muslim soil, while the relationships with Islamic civilization spawned some fascinating styles unique to Spain. The Moors adorned their towns with sensuous palaces, such as Granada's Alhambra, and elegant mosques, as well as employing compact climate-driven urban planning that still forms the hearts of most towns. In modern times Spain has shaken off the ponderous monumentalism of the Franco era and become something of a powerhouse of modern architecture.

Andalucía's finest early stone structures are in Antequera, whose dolmens are extraordinarily monumental burial spaces built from vast slabs of stone. The dwellings of the period were less permanent structures of which little evidence remains, except at the remarkable site of **Los Millares** near Almería, a large Chalcolithic settlement, necropolis, and sophisticated associated fortifications that has provided valuable information about society in the third millennium BC. The first millennium BC saw the construction of further fortified settlements, usually on hilltops. Little remains of this period in Andalucía, as the towns were then occupied by the Romans and Moors.

Similarly, while the Phoenicians established many towns in southern Spain, their remains are few; they were so adept at spotting natural harbours that nearly all have been in continual use ever since, leaving only the odd foundations or breakwater. There are also few Carthaginian remains of note. Their principal base in Andalucía was Cádiz, but two millennia of subsequent occupation have taken their toll on the archaeological record.

The story of Spanish architecture really begins with the Romans, who colonized the peninsula and imposed their culture on it to a significant degree. More significant still is the legacy they left; architectural principles that endured and to some extent formed the basis for later peninsular styles.

There's not a wealth of outstanding monuments; **Itálica**, just outside Sevilla, and **Baelo Claudia**, on the Costa de la Luz, are impressive, if not especially well-preserved Roman towns. **Acinipo**, near Ronda, has a large and spectacularly sited theatre, **Carmona** has a beautifully excavated necropolis and **Almuñécar** has the ruins of its fish sauce factory on display. In many towns and villages you can see Roman fortifications and foundations under existing structures.

There are few architectural reminders of the Visigothic period, although it was far from a time of lawless barbarism. Germanic elements were added to Roman and local traditions and there was widespread building; the kings of the period commissioned many churches, but in Andalucía these were all demolished to make way for mosques.

The first distinct period of Moorish architecture in Spain is that of the Umayyads who ruled as emirs, then as caliphs, from Córdoba from the eighth to 11th centuries. Although the Moors immediately set about building mosques, the earliest building still standing is Córdoba's **Mezquita**. Dating from the late ninth century, the ruined church at the mountain stronghold of Bobastro exhibits clear stylistic similarities with parts of the Mezquita and indicates that already a specifically *Andalusi* architecture was extant.

The period of the caliphate was the high point of Al-Andalus and some suitably sumptuous architecture remains. Having declared himself caliph, Abd al-Rahman III had the palace complex of **Madinat az-Zahra** built just outside of Córdoba. Now in ruins, excavation and reconstruction have revealed some of the one-time splendour, particularly of the throne room, which has arcades somewhat similar to those of the Mezquita and ornate relief designs depicting the Tree of Life and other vegetal motifs. The residential areas are centred around courtyards, a feature of Roman and Moorish domestic architecture that persists in Andalucía to this day.

The Mezquita had been added to by succeeding rulers, who enlarged it but didn't stray far from the original design. What is noticeable is a growing ornamentality, with use of multi-lobed arches, sometimes interlocking, and blind arcading on gateways. The *mihrab* was resituated and topped with a recessed dome, decorated with lavish mosaic work, possibly realized by Byzantine craftsmen. A less ornate mosque from this period can be seen in a beautiful hilltop setting at **Almonaster la Real** in the north of Huelva province.

Many defensive installations were also put up at this time: the castles of Tarifa and Baños de la Encina mostly date from this period. Bathhouses such as those of Jaén were also in use, although were modified in succeeding centuries. The typical Moorish *hammam* had a domed central space and vaulted chambers with star-shaped holes in the ceiling to admit natural light.

The *taifa* period, although politically chaotic, continued the rich architectural tradition of the caliphate. Málaga's **Alcazaba** preserved an 11th-century pavilion with delicate triple arches on slender columns. Elaborate stucco decoration, usually with repeating geometric or vegetal motifs, began to be used commonly during this time.

The Almoravids contributed little to Andalucían architecture, but the Almohads brought their own architectural modifications with them. Based in Sevilla, their styles were not as flamboyant and relied heavily on ornamental brickwork. The supreme example of the period is the **Giralda tower** that once belonged to the Mosque in Sevilla and now forms part of the cathedral. The use of intricate wood-panelled ceilings began to be popular and the characteristic Andalucían azulejo decorative tiles were first used at this time. Over this period the horseshoe arch developed a point. The Almohads were great military architects and built or improved a large number of walls, fortresses and towers; these often have characteristic pointed battlements. The **Torre del Oro** in Sevilla is one of the most famous and attractive examples.

The climax of Moorish architecture ironically came when Al-Andalus was already doomed and had been reduced to the emirate of Granada. Under the Nasrid rulers of that city the sublime **Alhambra** was constructed; a palace and pleasure garden that took elegance and sophistication in architecture to previously unseen levels. Nearly all the attention was focused on the interior of the buildings, which consisted of galleries and courtyards offset by water features and elegant gardens. The architectural high point of this and other buildings is the sheer intricacy of the stucco decoration in panels surrounding the windows and doorways. Another ennobling feature is *mocárabes*, a curious concave decoration of prisms placed in a cupola or ceiling and resembling natural crystal formations in caves. The Alcázar in Sevilla is also a good example of the period, though actually constructed in Christian Spain; it is very Nasrid in character and Granadan craftsmen certainly worked on it.

As the Christians gradually took back Andalucía, they introduced their own styles, developed in the north with substantial influence from France and Italy. The Romanesque barely features in Andalucía; it was the Gothic style that influenced post-Reconquista church building in the 13th, 14th and 15th centuries. It was combined with styles learned under the Moors to form an Andalucían fusion known as Gothic-*mudéjar*. Many of the region's churches are constructed on these lines, typically featuring a rectangular floor plan with a triple nave surrounded by pillars, a polygonal chancel and square chapels. Gothic exterior buttresses were used and many had a bell tower decorated with ornate brickwork reminiscent of the Giralda, which was also rebuilt during this period.

The Andalucían Gothic style differs from the rest of the peninsula in its basic principles. Whereas in the north, the 'more space, less stone, more light' philosophy pervaded, practical considerations demanded different solutions in the south. One of these was space; the cathedrals normally occupied the site of the former mosque, which had square ground plans and were hemmed in by other buildings. Another was defence – on the coast in particular, churches and cathedrals had to be ready to double as fortresses in case of attack, so sturdy walls were of more importance than stained glass. The redoubt of a cathedral at Almería is a typical example. Many of Andalucía's churches, built in the Gothic style, were heavily modified in succeeding centuries and present a blend of different architectures.

Mudéjar architecture spread quickly across Spain. Moorish architects and those who worked with them began to meld their Islamic tradition with the northern influences. The result is distinctive and pleasing, typified by the decorative use of brick and coloured tiles, with tall elegant bell towers a particular highlight. Another common feature is the highly elaborate wooden panelled ceilings, some of which are masterpieces. The word *artesonado* describes the most characteristic type of these. The style became popular nationwide; in certain areas, *mudéjar* remained a constant feature for over 500 years of building.

The final phase of Spanish Gothic was the Isabelline, or Flamboyant. Produced during and immediately after the reign of the Catholic Monarchs (hence the name), it borrowed decorative motifs from Islamic architecture to create an exuberant form characterized by highly elaborate façades carved with tendrils, sweeping curves and geometrical patterns. The Capilla Real in Granada is an example and the Palacio de Jabalquinto in Baeza is a superb demonstration of the style.

The 16th century was a high point in Spanish power and wealth, when it expanded across the Atlantic, tapping riches that must have seemed limitless. Spanish Renaissance architecture reflected this, leading from the late Gothic style into the elaborate peninsular style known as Plateresque. Although the style originally relied heavily on Italian models, it soon took on specifically Spanish features. The word refers particularly to the façades of civil and religious buildings, characterized by decoration of shields and other heraldic motifs, as well as geometric and naturalistic patterns such as shells. The term comes from the word for silversmith, *platero*, as the level of intricacy of the stonework approached that of jewellery. Arches went back to the rounded and columns and piers became a riot of foliage and 'grotesque' scenes.

A classical revival put an end to much of the elaboration, as Renaissance architects concentrated on purity. To classical Greek features such as fluted columns and pediments were added large Italianate cupolas and domes. Spanish architects were apprenticed to Italian masters and returned to Spain with their ideas. Elegant interior patios in *palacios* are an especially attractive feature of the style, to be found across the country. Andalucía is a particularly rich storehouse of this style, where the master Diego de Siloé designed numerous cathedrals and churches. The palace of Carlos V in the Alhambra grounds is often cited as one of the finest examples of Renaissance purity. One of Diego de Siloé's understudies, Andrés de Vandelvira, evolved into the über-architect of the Spanish Renaissance. The ensemble of palaces and churches he designed in Jaén province, particularly in the towns of Ubeda and Baeza, are unsurpassed in their sober beauty. Other fine 16th-century *palacios* can be found in nearly every town and city of Andalucía; often built in honey-coloured sandstone, these noble buildings were the homes of the aristocrats who had reaped the riches of the Reconquista and the new trade routes to the Americas.

The pure lines of this Renaissance classicism were soon to be transformed into a new style, Spanish Baroque. Although it started fairly soberly, it soon became rather ornamental, often being used to add elements to existing buildings. The Baroque was a time of great genius in architecture as in the other arts in Spain, as masters playfully explored the reaches of their imaginations; a strong reaction against the sober preceding style. Churches became ever larger, in part to justify the huge façades, and nobles indulged in one-upmanship, building ever-grander *palacios*. The façades themselves are typified by such features as pilasters (narrow piers descending to a point) and niches to hold statues. Andalucía has a vast array of Baroque churches; Sevilla in particular bristles with them, while Cádiz cathedral is almost wholly built in this style. Smaller towns, such as Priego de Córdoba and Ecija, are also well endowed, as they both enjoyed significant agriculture-based prosperity during the period.

The Baroque became more ornate as time went on, reaching the extremes of Churrigueresque, named for the Churriguera brothers who worked in the late 17th and early 18th centuries. The result can be overelaborate but on occasion transcendentally beautiful. Vine tendrils and cherubs decorate façades and *retablos*, which seem intent on breaking every classical norm, twisting here, upside-down there and at their best seeming to capture motion.

Neoclassicism, encouraged by a new interest in the ancient civilizations of Greece and Rome, was an inevitable reaction to such *joie de vivre*. It again resorted to the cleaner lines of antiquity, which were used this time for public spaces as well as civic and religious buildings. Many plazas and town halls in Spain are in this style, which tended to flourish in the cities that were thriving in the late 18th and 19th centuries, such as Cádiz, whose elegant old town is largely in this style. The best examples use symmetry to achieve beauty and elegance, such as the Prado in Madrid, or Sevilla's tobacco factory, which bridges Baroque and neoclassical styles.

The late 19th century saw Catalan *modernista* architecture break the moulds in a startling way. At the forefront of the movement was Antoni Gaudí. Essentially a highly original interpretation of art nouveau, Gaudí's style featured naturalistic curves and contours enlivened with stylistic elements inspired by Muslim and Gothic architecture. There is little *modernista* influence in Andalucía, but more sober *fin de siècle* architecture can be seen in Almería, which was a prosperous industrial powerhouse at the time.

Awakened interest in the days of Al-Andalus led to the neo-Moorish (or neo-*mudéjar*) style being used for public buildings and private residences. The most evident example of this is the fine ensemble of buildings constructed in Sevilla for the 1929 Ibero-American exhibition. Budgets were thrown out the window and the lavish pavilions are sumptuously decorated. Similarly ornate is the theatre in Cádiz.

Elegance and whimsy never seemed to play much part in fascist architecture and during the Franco era Andalucía was subjected to an appalling series of ponderous concrete monoliths, all in the name of progress. A few avant-garde buildings managed to escape the drudgery from the 1950s on, but it was the dictator's death in 1975, followed by EEC membership in 1986, that really provided the impetus for change.

Andalucía is not at the forefront of Spain's modern architectural movements, but the World Expo in Sevilla in 1992 brought some of the big names in. Among the various innovative pavilions, Santiago Calatrava's sublime bridges stand out. The impressive Teatro de la Maestranza and public library also date from this period, while the newer Olympic stadium, and Málaga's Picasso Museum and Centro de Arte Contemporáneo – both successful adaptations of older buildings – are more recent offerings. Sevilla's fantastic Parasol building, daringly built over a square in the old town, is the latest spectacular construction. Elsewhere, the focus has been on softening the harsh Francoist lines of the cities' 20th-century expansions. In most places this has been quietly successful. Much of the coast, however, is still plagued by the concrete curse, where planning laws haven't been strict enough in some places, and have been circumvented with a well-placed bribe in others.

In the first millennium BC, Iberian cultures produced fine jewellery from gold and silver, as well as some remarkable sculpture and ceramics.These influences derived from contact with trading posts set up by the Phoenicians, who also left artistic evidence of their presence, mostly in the port cities they established. Similarly, the Romans brought their own artistic styles to the peninsula and there are many cultural remnants, including some fine sculpture and a number of elaborate mosaic floors. Later, the Visigoths were skilled artists and craftspeople and produced many fine pieces, most notably in metalwork.

The majority of the artistic heritage left by the Moors is tied up in their architecture (see below). As Islamic tradition has tended to veer away from the portrayal of human or animal figures, the norm was intricate applied decoration with calligraphic, geometric and vegetal themes predominating. Superb panelled ceilings are a feature of Almohad architecture; a particularly attractive style being that known as *artesonado*, in which the concave panels are bordered with elaborate inlay work. During this period, glazed tiles known as *azulejos* began to be produced; these continue to be a feature of Andalucían craftsmanship.

The gradual process of the *Reconquista* brought Christian styles into Andalucía. Generally speaking, the Gothic, which had arrived in Spain both overland from France and across the Mediterranean from Italy, was the first post-Moorish style in Andalucía. Over time, Gothic sculpture achieved greater naturalism and became more ornate, culminating in the technical mastery of sculptors and painters, such as Pedro Millán, Pieter Dancart (who is responsible for the massive altarpiece of Sevilla's cathedral) and Alejo Fernández, all of whom were from or heavily influenced by northern Europe.

Though to begin with, the finest artists were working in Northern Spain, Andalucía soon could boast several notable figures of its own. In the wake of the Christian conquest of Granada, the Catholic Monarchs and their successor Carlos V went on a building spree. The Spanish Renaissance drew heavily on the Italian but developed its own style. Perhaps the finest 16th-century figure is Pedro de Campaña, a Fleming whose exalted talent went largely unrecognized in his own time. His altarpiece of the Purification of Mary in Sevilla's cathedral is particularly outstanding. The Italian sculptor Domenico Fancelli was entrusted by Carlos to carve the tombs of Fernando and Isabel in Granada; these are screened by a fine *reja* (grille) by Maestro Bartolomé, a Jaén-born artist who has several such pieces in Andalucían churches. The best-known 16th-century Spanish artist, the Cretan Domenikos Theotokopoulos (El Greco), has a few works in Andalucía, but the majority are in Toledo and Madrid.

As the Renaissance progressed, naturalism in painting increased, leading into the Golden Age of Spanish art. As Sevilla prospered on New World riches, the city became a centre for artists, who found wealthy patrons in abundance. Pre-eminent among all was Diego Rodríguez de Silva Velázquez (1599-1660), who started his career there before moving to Madrid to become a court painter. Another remarkable painter working in Sevilla was Francisco de Zurbarán

(1598-1664) whose idiosyncratic style often focuses on superbly rendered white garments in a dark, brooding background, a metaphor for the subjects themselves, who were frequently priests. During Zurbarán's later years, he was eclipsed in the Sevilla popularity stakes by Bartolomé Esteban Murillo (1618-1682). While at first glance his paintings can seem heavy on the sentimentality, they tend to focus on the space between the central characters, who interact with glances or gestures of great power and meaning. Juan Valdés Leal painted many churches and monasteries in Sevilla; his greatest works are the macabre realist paintings in the Hospital de la Caridad. The sombre tone struck by these works reflects the decline of the once-great mercantile city.

At this time, the sculptor Juan Martínez Montañés carved numerous figures, *retablos* and *pasos* (ornamental floats for religious processions) in wood. Pedro Roldán, Juan de Mesa and Pedro de Mena were other important Baroque sculptors from this period, as was Alonso Cano, a crotchety but talented painter and sculptor working from Granada. The main focus of this medium continued to be ecclesiastic; *retablos* became ever larger and more ornate, commissioned by nobles to gain favour with the church and improve their chances in the afterlife.

The 18th and early 19th centuries saw fairly characterless art produced under the new dynasty of Bourbon kings. Tapestry production increased markedly but never scaled the heights of the earlier Flemish masterpieces. One man who produced pictures for tapestries was the master of 19th-century art, Francisco Goya. Goya was a remarkable figure whose finest works included both paintings and etchings; there's a handful of his work scattered around Andalucía's galleries, but the best examples are in Madrid's Prado and in the north.

After Goya, the 19th century produced few works of note as Spain tore itself apart in a series of brutal wars and conflicts. Perhaps in reaction to this, the *costumbrista* tradition developed; these painters and writers focused on portraying Spanish life; their depictions often revolving around nostalgia and stereotypes. Among the best were the Bécquer family: José; his cousin Joaquín; and his son Valeriano, whose brother Gustavo Adolfo was one of the period's best-known poets.

The early 20th century saw the rise of Spanish modernism and surrealism, much of it driven from Catalunya. While architects such as Gaudí managed to combine their discipline with art, it was one man from Málaga who had such an influence on 20th-century painting that he is arguably the most famous artist in the world. Pablo Ruiz Picasso (1881-1973) is notable not just for his artistic genius, but also for his evolution through different styles. Training in Barcelona, but doing much of his work in Paris, his initial Blue Period was fairly sober and subdued, named for predominant use of that colour. His best early work, however, came in his succeeding Pink Period, where he used brighter tones to depict the French capital. He moved on from this to become a pioneer of cubism. Drawing on non-western forms, cubism forsook realism for a new form of three-dimensionality, trying to show subjects from as many different angles as possible. Picasso then moved on to more surrealist forms. He continued painting right throughout his lifetime and produced an incredible number of works. One of his best-known paintings is *Guernica*, a nightmarish ensemble of terror-struck animals and people that he produced in abhorrence of the Nationalist bombing of the defenceless Basque market town in April 1937. The Picasso Museum in Málaga displays a range of his works.

A completely different contemporary was the Córdoban Julio Romero de Torres, a painter who specialized in sensuous depictions of Andalucían women, usually fairly unencumbered by clothing. A more sober 20th-century painter was Daniel Vázquez Díaz, a Huelvan who adorned the walls of La Rábida monastery with murals on the life of Columbus.

The Civil War was to have a serious effect on art in Spain, as a majority of artists sided with the Republic and fled Spain with their defeat. Franco was far from an enlightened patron of the arts and his occupancy was a monotonous time. Times have changed, however, and the regional governments, including the Andalucían, are extremely supportive of local artists these days and the museums in each provincial capital usually have a good collection of modern works.

Literature

The peninsula's earliest known writers lived under the Roman occupation. Of these, two of the best known hailed from Córdoba; Seneca the Younger (3 BC-AD 65), the Stoic poet, philosopher and statesman who lived most of his life in Rome, and his nephew Lucan (AD 39-AD 65), who is known for his verse history of the wars between Caesar and Pompey, *Bellum Civile*. Both were forced to commit suicide for plotting against the emperor Nero. After the fall of Rome, one of the most remarkable of all Spain's literary figures was the bishop of Sevilla, San Isidoro, whose works were classic texts for over a millennium, see box, page 69.

In Al-Andalus a flourishing literary culture existed under the Córdoba caliphate and later. Many important works were produced by Muslim and Jewish authors; some were to have a large influence on European knowledge and thought. The writings of Ibn Rushd (Averroes; 1126-1198) were of fundamental importance, asserting that the study of philosophy was not incompatible with religion and commentating extensively on Aristotle; see box, opposite. The discovery of his works a couple of centuries on by Christian scholars led to the rediscovery of Aristotle and played a triggering role in the Renaissance. His contemporary in Córdoba, Maimonides (1135-1204) was one of the foremost Jewish writers of all time; writing on Jewish law, religion and spirituality in general and medicine, he remains an immense and much-studied figure; see box, opposite. Another important Jewish writer was the philosopher and poet Judah ha-Levi (1075-1141); although born in the north, he spent much of his time writing in Granada and Córdoba. Throughout the Moorish period, there were many chronicles, treatises and studies written by Arab authors, but poetry was the favoured form of literary expression. Well-crafted verses, often about love and frequently quite explicit, were penned by such authors as the Sevilla king Al-Mu'tamid and the Córdoban Ibn Hazm.

After the Moors, however, Andalucía didn't really produce any literature of note until the so-called Golden Age of Spanish writing, which came in the wake of the

BACKGROUND
Averroes and Maimonides

Two of Córdoba's most famous sons, and scholars of immense historical significance, were born within a few years of each other in the city in the 12th century.

Ibn Rushd, better known as Averroes (1126-1198), was from a high-ranking Moorish family. An extraordinary polymath, he was a doctor, theologian, philosopher, mathematician and lawyer. He was well respected by the rulers of Córdoba until a backlash against philosophers saw him banished to Morocco and many of his texts burned. Averroes' primary thesis was that the study of philosophy was not incompatible with religion. He commentated extensively on Aristotle and the rediscovery of some of these works played a triggering role in the Christian Renaissance.

Moses Maimonides (Moses ben Maimun; 1135-1204) was born of Jewish parents in Córdoba, but moved on at a fairly young age, finishing up in Cairo. Like Averroes, he was a physician, and became an absolute authority on Jewish law, religion, and spirituality. He wrote several commentaries on the ancient Hebrew texts; such was his influence that it has been said that "Between Moses and Moses, there was no one like unto Moses". As with Averroes, he had a great influence on the development of philosophy in succeeding centuries.

discovery of the Americas and the flourishing of trade and wealth; patronage was crucial for writers in those days. The most notable poet of the period is the Córdoban Luis de Góngora (1561-1627), whose exaggerated, affected style is deeply symbolic (and sometimes almost inaccessible). His work has been widely appreciated recently and critics tend to label him the greatest of all Spanish poets, though he still turns quite a few people off.

The extraordinary life of Miguel de Cervantes (1547-1616) marks the start of a rich period of Spanish literature. *Don Quijote* came out in serial form in 1606 and is rightly considered one of the finest novels ever written; it's certainly the widest-read Spanish work. Cervantes spent plenty of time in Andalucía and some of his *Novelas Ejemplares* are short stories set in Sevilla.

The Sevillian, Lope de Rueda (1505-1565), was in many ways Spain's first playwright. He wrote comedies and paved the way for the explosion of Spanish drama under the big three – Lope de Vega, Tirso de la Molina and Calderón de la Barca – when public theatres opened in the early 17th century.

The 18th century was not such a rich period for Andalucían or Spanish writing but in the 19th century the *costumbrista* movement (see page 91) produced several fine works, among them *La Gaviota* (the Seagull), by Fernán Caballero, who was actually a Sevilla-raised woman named Cecilia Böhl von Faber, and *Escenas Andaluzas* (Andalucían Scenes), by Serafín Estébanez Calderón. Gustavo Adolfo Bécquer died young having published a famous series of legends and just one volume of poetry, popular, yearning works about love. Pedro Antonio de Alarcón

BACKGROUND

Antonio Machado

Mi infancia son recuerdos de un patio de Sevilla, / y un huerto claro donde madura el limonero; / mi juventud, veinte años en tierras de Castilla; / mi historia, algunos casos que recordar no quiero

My childhood is memories of a patio in Sevilla, / and of a light-filled garden where the lemon tree grows / My youth, twenty years in the lands of Castilla / My story, some happenings I wish not to remember

Along with Federico García Lorca, Antonio Machado was Spain's greatest 20th-century poet. Part of the so-called Generation of '98 who struggled to re-evaluate Spain in the wake of losing its last colonial possessions in 1898, he was born in 1875 in Sevilla.

Growing up mostly in Madrid, he spent time in France and then lived and worked in Soria, in Castilla; much of his poetry is redolent of the harsh landscapes of that region. His solitude was exacerbated when his young wife Leonor died after three years of marriage. He then moved to Baeza, where he taught French in a local school. Like the poetry written in Soria, his work in Andalucía reflected his profound feelings for the landscape.

Machado was a staunch defender of the Republic and became something of a bard of the Civil War. Forced to flee with thousands of refugees as the Republic fell, he died not long after, in 1939, in a pensión in southern France. His will to live was dealt a bitter blow by the triumph of fascism, while his health had suffered badly during the trying journey.

(1833-1901), who hailed from Guadix, is most famous for his work *The Three-Cornered Hat*, a light and amusing tale which draws heavily on Andalucían customs and characters; it was also made into a popular ballet.

At the end of the 19th century, Spain lost the last of its colonial possessions after revolts and a war with the USA. This event, known as the Disaster, had a profound impact on the nation and its date 1898 gave its name to a generation of writers and artists. This group sought to express what Spain was and had been and to achieve new perspectives for the 20th century. One of their number was Antonio Machado (1875-1939), one of Spain's greatest poets; see box, above.

Another excellent poet of this time was Juan Ramón Jiménez (1881-1958), from Moguer in Huelva province, who won the Nobel Prize in 1956. His best-known work is the long prose poem *Platero y Yo*, a lyrical portrait of the town and the region conducted as a conversation between the writer and his donkey. He was forced into exile by the Spanish Civil War.

The Granadan Federico García Lorca was a young poet and playwright of great ability and lyricism with a gypsy streak in his soul. His play *Bodas de Sangre* (Blood Wedding) sits among the finest Spanish drama ever written and his verse ranges from the joyous to the haunted and draws heavily on Andalucían folk traditions.

Lorca was shot by fascist thugs in Granada just after the outbreak of hostilities in the Civil War; one of the most poignant of the thousands of atrocities committed in that bloody conflict.

Lorca was associated with the so-called Generation of 27, another loose grouping of artists and writers. One of their number was Rafael Alberti (1902-1999), a poet from El Puerto de Santa María and a close friend of Lorca's. Achieving recognition with his first book of poems, *Mar y Tierra*, Alberti was a Communist (who once met Stalin) and fought on the Republican side in the Civil War. He was forced into exile at the end of the war, only returning to Spain in 1978. Other Andalucían poets associated with this movement were the neo-romantic Luis Cernuda (1902-1963) and Vicente Aleixandre (1898-1984), winner of the 1977 Nobel Prize for his surrealist-influenced free verse. Both men were from Sevilla.

Although Aleixandre stayed in Spain, despite his poems being banned for a decade, the exodus and murder of the country's most talented writers was a heavy blow for literature. The greatest novelists of the Franco period, Camilo José Cela and Miguel Delibes, both hailed from the north, but in more recent times Andalucía has come to the fore again with Antonio Múnoz Molina (born 1956) from Ubeda in Jaén province. His *Ardor Guerrero* (*Warrior Lust*) is a bitter look at military service, while his highly acclaimed *Sepharad* is a collection of interwoven stories broadly about the Diaspora and Jewish Spain and set in various locations ranging from concentration camps to rural Andalucían villages. In 2013 he won the prestigious Prince of Asturias prize, Spain's top literary award.

Music and dance

Flamenco

Few things symbolize the mysteries of Andalucía like flamenco but, as with the region itself, much has been written that is over-romanticized, patronizing or just plain untrue. Like bullfighting, flamenco as we know it is a fairly young art, having basically developed in the 19th century. It is constantly evolving and there have been significant changes in its performance in the last century, which makes the search for classic flamenco a bit of a wild goose chase. Rather, the element to search for is authentic emotion and, beyond this, *duende*, an undefinable passion that carries singer and watchers away in a whirlwind of raw feeling, with a devil-may-care sneer at destiny.

Though there have been many excellent *payo* flamenco artists, its history is primarily a gypsy one. It was developed among the gypsy population in the Sevilla and Cádiz area but clearly includes elements of cultures encountered further away.

Flamenco consists of three basic components: *el cante* (the song), *el toque* (the guitar) and *el baile* (the dance). In addition, *el jaleo* provides percussion sounds through shouts, clicking fingers, clapping and footwork (and, less traditionally, castanets). Flamenco can be divided into four basic types: *tonás*, *siguiriyas*, *soleá* and *tangos*, which are characterized by their *comps* or form, rhythm and accentuation and are either *cante jondo* (emotionally deep)/*cante grande* (big) or *cante ligero* (lighter)/*cante chico* (small). Related to flamenco, but not in a pure form, are *sevillanas*, danced till you drop at Feria, and *rocieras*, which are sung on (and about) the annual *romería* pilgrimage to El Rocío.

For a foreigner, perhaps the classic image of flamenco is a woman in a theatrical dress clicking castanets. A more authentic image is of a singer and guitarist, both sitting rather disconsolately on ramshackle chairs, or perhaps on a wooden box to tap out a rhythm. The singer and the guitarist work together, sensing the mood of the other and improvising. A beat is provided by clapping of hands or tapping of feet. If there's a dancer, he or she will lock into the mood of the others and vice versa. The dancing is stop-start, frenetic: the flamenco can reach crescendoes of frightening intensity when it seems the singer will have a stroke, the dancer is about to commit murder, and the guitarist may never find it back to the world of the sane. These outbursts of passion are seen to their fullest in *cante jondo*, the deepest and saddest form of flamenco.

After going through a moribund period during the mid-20th century, flamenco was revived by such artists as Paco de Lucía, and the gaunt, heroin-addicted genius Camarón de la Isla, while the flamenco theatre of Joaquín Cortés put purists' noses firmly out of joint but achieved worldwide popularity. More recently, Diego 'El Cigala' carries on Camarón's angst-ridden tradition. Fusions of flamenco with other styles have been a feature of recent years, with the flamenco-rock of Ketama and the flamenco-chillout of Málaga-based Chambao achieving notable success. Granada's late Enrique Morente, a flamenco artist from the old school, outraged purists with his willingness to experiment with other artists and musical forms; his release Omega brought in a punk band to accompany him and featured flamenco covers of Leonard Cohen hits.

Other music

Music formed a large part of cultural life in the days of the Córdoba emirate and caliphate. The earliest known depiction of a lute comes from an ivory bottle dated around AD 968; the musician Ziryab, living in the 11th century, made many important modifications to the lute, including the addition of a fifth double-string.

Like other art forms, music enjoyed something of a golden age under the early Habsburg monarchs. It was during this period that the five-string Spanish guitar came to be developed and the emergence of a separate repertoire for this instrument.

In 1629 Lope de Vega wrote the libretto for the first Spanish opera, which was to become a popular form. A particular Spanish innovation was the *zarzuela*, a musical play with speech and dancing. It became widely popular in the 19th century and is still performed in the larger cities. Spain's contribution to opera has been very important and has produced in recent times a number of world-class singers such as Montserrat Caballé, Plácido Domingo, José Carreras and Teresa Berganza.

The Cádiz-born Manuel de Falla is the greatest figure in the history of a country that has produced few classical composers. He drew heavily on Andalucían themes and culture and also helped keep flamenco traditions alive.

De Falla's friendship with Debussy in Paris led to the latter's work *Ibéria*, which, although the Frenchman never visited Spain, was described by Lorca as very evocative of Andalucía. It was the latest of many Andalucía-inspired compositions, which include Bizet's *Carmen*, from the story by Prosper Merimée and Rossini's *The Barber of Seville*, based on the play by Beaumarchais.

Contemporary music

Flamenco aside, Andalucía doesn't have a cutting-edge contemporary music scene. Most bars and *discotecas* play a repetitive selection of Spanish pop, much of it derived from the phenomenally successful TV show *Operación Triunfo*, a star-creation programme that spawned *Fame Academy* in the UK.

In contrast, the Andalucían Joaquín Sabina is a heavyweight singer-songwriter who works both solo and in collaboration with other musicians. His songs draw on Andalucían folk traditions and he is deeply critical of modern popular culture. His gravelly voice is distinctive and has deservedly won him worldwide fame.

Practicalities
Málaga

Getting there

There are numerous options for reaching Málaga. Málaga airport is served regularly by flights from a wide variety of European cities; add in all the standard and charter flights, and it's one of Europe's easiest destinations to reach.

Charter flights are cheaper and are run by package holiday firms. You can find bargains through travel agencies or online. The drawback of these flights is that they usually have a fixed return flight, often only a week or a fortnight later, and they frequently depart at antisocial hours. An upside is that charter flights operate from many regional airports.

Before booking, it's worth doing a bit of online research. Three of the best search engines for flight comparisons are www.opodo.com, www.skyscanner.com and www.kayak.com, which compare prices from a range of agencies. To keep up to date with the ever-changing routes available, sites like www.flightmapper.net are handy. Flightchecker (http://flightchecker.moneysavingexpert.com) is handy for checking multiple dates for budget airline deals.

Flights from the UK
Competition has benefited travellers in recent years. Budget operators have taken a significant slice of the market and forced other airlines to compete.

Budget There are numerous budget connections from the UK to Málaga. **Easyjet** and **Ryanair** connect Málaga with over a dozen UK airports, while other budget airlines running various routes from the UK to Málaga include **Flybe**, **Vueling**, **Norwegian**, **Jet2**, **Thomson** and **Monarch**.

Charter There are numerous charter flights to Málaga from many British and Irish airports. **Avro** ⓘ *www.avro.co.uk*, **Thomas Cook** ⓘ *www.thomascook.com*, and **Thomson** ⓘ *www.thomson.co.uk*, are some of the best charter flight providers, but it's also worth checking the travel pages of newspapers for cheap deals. The website www.flightsdirect.com is also a good tool to search for charter flights.

Non-budget flights Málaga has scheduled flights with several airlines including **Iberia** and **British Airways** flying direct from London airports and a few other UK cities.

Flights from the rest of Europe
There are numerous budget airlines operating from European and Spanish cities to Málaga.

Numerous charter flights operate to Málaga from Germany, Scandinavia, France, the Netherlands and Belgium.

There are non-stop flights to Málaga with non-budget airlines from many major European cities. Flying from western European cities via Madrid or Barcelona usually costs about the same.

Flights from North America and Canada

Delta fly direct from New York to Málaga, while there are fortnightly charter flights from Montreal and Toronto with **Air Transat**. Otherwise, you'll have to connect via Madrid, Barcelona, Lisbon, London or another European city. Although sometimes you'll pay little extra to Andalucía than the Madrid flight, you can often save considerably by flying to Madrid and getting the bus down south or book a domestic connection on the local no-frills airline **Vueling** ⓘ www.vueling.com, or **Ryanair** ⓘ www.ryanair.com.

Flights from Australia and New Zealand

There are no direct flights to Spain from Australia or New Zealand; the cheapest and quickest way is to connect via Frankfurt, Paris or London. It might turn out cheaper to book the Europe–Spain leg separately via a budget operator.

Road

Bus

Eurolines ⓘ T01582-404511, www.eurolines.com, runs several buses from major European cities to Málaga, but you won't get there cheaper than a flight.

Car and sea

It's a long haul to Málaga by road if you're not already in the peninsula. From the UK, you have two options if you want to take the car: take a ferry to northern Spain (www.brittany-ferries.co.uk), or cross the Channel to France and then drive down. The former option is much more expensive; it would usually work out far cheaper to fly to Málaga and hire a car once you get there. For competitive fares by sea to France and Spain, check with **Ferrysavers** ⓘ www.ferrysavers.com, or **Direct Ferries** ⓘ www.directferries.com.

Málaga is about 2000 km from London by road; a dedicated drive will get you there in 20-24 driving hours. By far the fastest route is to head down the west coast of France and to Burgos via San Sebastián. From here, head south via Madríd.

Train

Unless you've got a rail pass, love train travel or aren't too keen on planes, forget about getting to Málaga by train from anywhere further than France; you'll save no money over the plane fare and use up days of time better spent in tapas bars. You'll have to connect via either Barcelona or Madrid. Getting to Madrid/Barcelona from London takes about a day using **Eurostar** ⓘ *www.eurostar.com, £100-250 return to Paris, and another €130 or more return to reach Madrid/Barcelona from there.* Using the train/Channel ferry combination will more or less halve the cost and double the time to Paris.

If you are planning the train journey, **Voyages-SNCF** ⓘ *www.voyages-sncf. com*, is a useful company. RENFE, Spain's rail network, has online timetables at www.renfe.com. Best of all is the extremely useful www.seat61.com.

Getting around

Public transport between the cities of Andalucía is good, with lots of bus services, and several fast train connections.

Road

Bus

Buses are the staple of Spanish public transport. Services between major cities are fast, frequent, reliable and fairly cheap. When buying a ticket, always check how long the journey will take, as the odd bus will be an 'all stations to' job, calling in at villages that seem surprised to even see it.

Most cities have a single terminal, the *estación de autobuses*. Buy your tickets at the relevant window; if there isn't one, buy it from the driver. Superior classes may cost up to 60% more but offer lounge access and onboard service. Newer buses in all classes may offer Wi-Fi, personal entertainment system and sockets. Most tickets will have an *asiento* (seat number) on them; ask when buying the ticket if you prefer a *ventana* (window) or *pasillo* (aisle) seat. Some of the companies allow booking online or by phone. If you're travelling at busy times (particularly a fiesta or national holiday) always book the bus ticket in advance.

Rural bus services are slower, less frequent and more difficult to coordinate.

All bus services are reduced on Sundays and, to a lesser extent, on Saturdays; some services don't run at all on weekends.

Car

Roads and motorways The roads in Andalucía are good, excellent in many parts. While driving isn't as sedate as in parts of northern Europe, it's generally pretty good and you'll have few problems. The roads near the coast, dense with partygoers and sunseekers, can be dangerous in summer, particularly the stretch along the Costa del Sol.

There are two types of motorway in Spain, *autovías* and *autopistas*; for drivers, they are little different. They are signposted in blue and may have tolls payable, in which case there'll be a red warning circle on the blue sign when you're entering the motorway. Tolls are generally reasonable; the quality of motorway is generally excellent. The speed limit on motorways is 120 kph, though it is scheduled to rise to 130 kph on some stretches.

Rutas Nacionales form the backbone of the country's road network. Centrally administered, they vary wildly in quality. Typically, they are choked with traffic backed up behind trucks, and there are few stretches of dual carriageway. Driving at siesta time is a good idea if you're going to be on a busy stretch. *Rutas Nacionales* are marked with a red N followed by a number. The speed limit is 100 kph outside built-up areas, as it is for secondary roads, which are usually marked with an A (Andalucía), or C (*comarcal*, or local) prefix.

In urban areas, the speed limit is 50 kph. City driving can be confusing, with signposting generally poor and traffic heavy; it's worth using a Satnav or printing off the directions that your hotel may send you with a reservation. In some towns and cities, many of the hotels are officially signposted, making things easier. Larger cities may have their historic quarter blocked off by barriers; if your hotel lies within these, ring the buzzer and say the name of the hotel, and the barriers will open. Other cities enforce restrictions by camera, so you'll have to give your number plate details to the hotel so they can register it.

Police are increasingly enforcing speed limits in Spain, and foreign drivers are liable to a large on-the-spot fine. Drivers can also be punished for not carrying two red warning triangles to place on the road in case of breakdown, a bulb-replacement kit and a fluorescent green waistcoat to wear if you break down by the side of the road. Drink driving is being cracked down on; the limit is 0.5 g/l of blood, a little lower than the equivalent in the UK, for example.

Parking Parking is a problem in nearly every town and city in Andalucía. Red or yellow lines on the side of the street mean no parking. Blue or white lines mean that some restrictions are in place; a sign will indicate what these are (typically it means that the parking is metered). Parking meters can usually only be dosed up for a maximum of two hours, but they take a siesta at lunchtime too. Print the ticket off and display it in the car. If you overstay and get fined, you can pay it off for minimal cost at the machine if you do it within an hour of the fine being issued. Parking fines are never pursued for foreign vehicles, but if it's a hire car you'll likely be liable for it. Underground car parks are common, but pricey; €15-20 a day is normal. The website www.parkopedia.es is useful for locating underground car parks and comparing their rates.

Documentation To drive in Spain, you'll need a full driving licence from your home country. This applies to virtually all foreign nationals but, in practice, if you're from an 'unusual' country, consider an International Driving Licence or official translation of your licence into Spanish.

Liability insurance is required for every car driven in Spain and you must carry proof of it. If bringing your own car, check carefully with your insurers that you're covered and get a certificate (green card).

Car hire Hiring a car in Málaga is easy and cheap. The major multinationals have offices at all large towns and airports. Prices start at around €150 per week for a small car with unlimited mileage. You'll need a credit card and most agencies will either not accept under-25s or demand a surcharge. By far the cheapest place to hire a car is Málaga, where even at the airport there are competitive rates. With the bigger companies, it's always cheaper to book over the internet. The best way to look for a deal is using a price-comparison website like www.kayak.com. Drop-offs in other cities, which used to be ridiculously punitive, are now often much more affordable.

There are often hidden charges, the most common being compulsory purchase of a tank of petrol at an overpriced rate. You then have to return the car with the tank empty.

Cycling and motorcycling

Motorcycling is a good way to enjoy Málaga and there are few difficulties to trouble the biker; bike shops and mechanics are relatively common. There are comparatively few outlets for motorcycle hire.

Cycling presents a curious contrast; Spaniards are mad for the competitive sport, but essentially disinterested in cycling as a means of transport, though local governments are trying to encourage it with new bike lanes and free borrowable bikes in cities. Thus there are plenty of cycling shops but few cycle-friendly features on the roads. Taking your own bike to Málaga is well worth the effort as most airlines are happy to accept them, providing they come within your baggage allowance. Bikes can be taken on the train, but have to travel in the guard's van and must be registered.

Hitchhiking

Hitchhiking is fairly easy in Spain, although not much practised. The police aren't too keen on it, but with sensible placement and a clearly written sign, you'll usually get a lift without a problem, particularly in rural areas, where, in the absence of bus services, it's a more common way for locals to get about.

Taxi and bus

Most Andalucían cities have their sights closely packed into the centre, so you won't find local buses particularly necessary. There's a fairly comprehensive network in most towns, though; the travel text indicates where they come in handy. Taxis are a good option; the minimum charge is around €2.50 in most places (it increases slightly at night and on Sundays). A taxi is available if its green light is lit; hail one on the street, call, or ask for the nearest *parada de taxis* (rank). If you're using a cab to get to somewhere beyond the city limits, there are fixed tariffs.

Train

The Spanish national rail network, RENFE ⓘ *T902-240202 (English-speaking operators), www.renfe.com for timetables and tickets*, is, thanks to its growing network of high-speed trains, a useful option. AVE trains run from Madrid to Málaga and, though expensive, cover these large distances impressively quickly and reliably. Elsewhere in Málaga though, you'll find the bus is often quicker and cheaper.

Prices vary significantly according to the type of service you are using. The standard high-speed intercity service is called *Talgo*, while other intercity services are labelled *Altaria*, *Intercity*, *Diurno* and *Estrella* (overnight). Slower local trains are called *regionales*. Alvia is a mixed AVE-Talgo service.

It's always worth buying a ticket in advance for long-distance travel, as trains are often full. The best option is to buy them via the website, which sometimes offers advance purchase discounts. The website is notoriously unreliable, with not all services appearing, and a clunky mechanism for finding connections. You can print out the ticket yourself, or print it at a railway station using the reservation code. If buying your ticket at the station, allow plenty of time for queuing. Ticket windows are labelled *venta anticipada* (in advance) and *venta inmediata* (six hours or less before the journey).

All Spanish trains are non-smoking. The faster trains will have a first-class (*preferente*) and second-class sections as well as a cafeteria. First class costs about 30% more than standard and can be a worthwhile deal on a crowded long journey. Families and groups can take advantage of the cheap 'mesa' tickets, where you reserve four seats around a table. Buying a return ticket is 10% to 20% cheaper than two singles, but you qualify for this discount even if you buy the return leg later (but not on every service).

An **ISIC student card** or **youth card** grants a discount of 20% to 25% on train services. If you're using a European railpass, be aware that you'll still have to make a reservation on Spanish trains and pay the small reservation fee (which covers your insurance). If you have turned 60, it's worth paying €6 for a Tarjeta Dorada, a seniors' card that gets you a discount of 40% on trains from Monday to Thursday, and 25% at other times.

Maps

A useful website for route planning is www.guiarepsol.com. Car hire companies have Satnavs available, though they cost a hefty supplement.

Where to stay

from casas rurales to campsites

The standard of accommodation in Málaga is very high; even the most modest of *pensiones* is usually very clean and respectable. At time of writing, for Spain the website www.booking.com is by far the most comprehensive. If you're booking accommodation not listed in this guide, always be sure to check the location if that's important to you – it's easy to find yourself a 15-minute cab ride from the town you think you're going to be in.

Environmental issues are an individual's responsibility, and the type of holiday you choose has a direct impact on the future of the region. Opting for more sustainable tourism choices – picking a *casa rural* in a traditional village and eating in restaurants serving locally sourced food rather than staying in the four-star multinational hotel – has a small but significant knock-on effect. Don't be afraid to ask questions about environmental policy before making a hotel or *casa rural* booking.

Types of accommodation

Alojamientos (places to stay), are divided into two main categories; the distinctions between them are in an arcane series of regulations devised by the government.

Hotels, hostales and pensiones

Hoteles (marked H or HR) are graded from one to five stars and occupy their own building, which distinguishes them from many *hostales* (Hs or HsR), which go from one to two stars. The *hostal* category includes *pensiones*, the standard budget option, typically family-run and occupying a floor of an apartment building. The standard for the price paid is normally excellent, and they're nearly all spotless. Spanish traditions of hospitality are alive and well; check-out time is almost uniformly a very civilized midday.

A great number of Spanish hotels are well equipped but characterless chain business places (big players include **NH** ⓘ *www.nh-hoteles.es*, **Husa** ⓘ *www.husa.es*, **AC/Marriott** ⓘ *www.marriott.com*, **Tryp/SolMelia**

Price codes

Where to stay	Restaurants
€€€€ over €170	€€€ over €30
€€€ €110-170	€€ €15-30
€€ €60-110	€ under €15
€ under €60	
A standard double/twin room in high season.	A two-course meal (or two average *raciones*) for one person, without drinks.

ⓘ *www.solmelia.com*, and **Riu** ⓘ *www.riu.com*). This guide has expressly minimized these in the listings, preferring to concentrate on more atmospheric options.

Casas rurales

An excellent option if you've got your own transport are the networks of rural houses, called *casas rurales*. Although these are under a different classification system, the standard is often as high as any country hotel. The best of them are traditional farmhouses or characterful village cottages. Some are available only to rent out whole (often for a minimum of three days), while others offer rooms on a nightly basis. Rates tend to be excellent compared to hotels. While many are listed in the text, there are huge numbers of them. Local tourist offices will have details of nearby *casas rurales*; the tourist board website www.andalucia.org lists a good selection.

Youth hostels

There's a network of *albergues* (youth hostels), which are listed at www.inturjoven. com. These are institutional and often group-booked. Funding issues mean that many now open only seasonally. Major cities have backpacker hostels with instant social life and every mod con. *Refugios* are mountain bunkhouses, which range from unstaffed sheds to cheerful hostels with a bar and restaurant.

Campsites

Most campsites are set up as well-equipped holiday villages for families; some are open only in summer. While the facilities are good, they get extremely busy in peak season. Many have cabins or bungalows available, ranging from simple huts to houses with fully equipped kitchens and bathrooms. In other areas, camping, unless specifically prohibited, is a matter of common sense. Don't camp where you're not allowed to; prohibitions are usually there for a good reason. Fire danger can be high in summer, so respect local regulations.

Prices

Price codes refer to a standard double or twin room, inclusive of VAT. The rates are generally for high season (June-August on the coast, March-May in cities). Occasionally, an area or town will have a short period when prices are hugely exaggerated; this is usually due to a festival.

Breakfast is often included in the price at small intimate hotels, but rarely at the grander places, who tend to charge a fortune. Normally only the more expensive hotels have parking, and they always charge for it, normally around €10-25 per day.

All registered accommodation charge a 10% value added tax; this is usually included in the price and may be waived if you pay cash. If you have any problems, a last resort is to ask for the *libro de reclamaciones* (complaints book), an official document that, like stepping on cracks in the pavement, means uncertain but definitely horrible consequences for the hotel if anything is written in it. Be aware that you must also take a copy to the local police station for the complaint to be registered.

Food & drink

In no country in the world are culture and society as intimately connected with eating and drinking as in Spain, and in Andalucía, the spiritual home of tapas, this is even more the case.

Food → *See page 124 for a glossary of food.*

Andalucían cooking is characterized by an abundance of fresh ingredients, generally consecrated with the chef's holy trinity of garlic, peppers and local olive oil.

Spaniards eat little for breakfast and, apart from hotels in touristy places, you're unlikely to find anything beyond a *tostada* (large piece of toasted bread spread with olive oil, tomato and garlic, pâté or jam) or a pastry to go with your coffee. A common breakfast or afternoon snack are *churros*, fried dough sticks typically dipped in hot chocolate.

Lunch is the main meal and is nearly always a filling affair with three courses. Most places open for lunch at about 1300, and take last orders at 1500 or 1530, although at weekends this can extend. Lunchtime is the cheapest time to eat if you opt for the ubiquitous *menú del día*, usually a set three-course meal that includes wine or soft drink, typically costing €10 to €16. Dinner and/or evening tapas time is from around 2100 to midnight. It's not much fun sitting alone in a restaurant so try and adapt to the local hours; it may feel strange dining so late, but you'll miss out on a lot of atmosphere if you don't. If a place is open for lunch at noon, or dinner at 1900, it's likely to be a tourist trap.

Types of eateries

The great joy of eating out in Málaga is going for tapas. This word refers to bar food, served in saucer-sized tapa portions typically costing €1.50-3. Tapas are available at lunchtime, but the classic time to eat them is in the evening. To do tapas the Andalucían way don't order more than a couple at each place, taste each others' dishes, and stand at the bar. Locals know what the specialities of each bar are; if there's a daily special, order that. Also available are *raciones*, substantial meal-sized plates of the same fare, which also come in halves, *medias raciones*. Both are good for sharing. Considering these, the distinction between restaurants and tapas bars more or less disappears, as in the latter you can usually sit down at a table to order your *raciones*, effectively turning the experience into a meal.

Other types of eateries include the *chiringuito*, a beach bar open in summer and serving drinks and fresh seafood. A *freiduría* is a takeaway specializing in fried fish, while a *marisquería* is a classier type of seafood restaurant. In rural areas, look out for *ventas*, roadside eateries that often have a long history of feeding the passing muleteers with generous, hearty and cheap portions. The more cars and trucks outside, the better it will be. In Málaga city, North African-style teahouses, *teterías*, are popular.

Vegetarian food

Vegetarians won't be spoiled for choice, but at least what there is tends to be good. There are few dedicated vegetarian restaurants and many restaurants won't have a vegetarian main course on offer, although the existence of tapas, *raciones* and salads makes this less of a burden than it might be. You'll have to specify *soy vegetariano/a* (I am a vegetarian), but ask what dishes contain, as ham, fish and even chicken are often considered suitable vegetarian fare. Vegans will have a tougher time. What doesn't have meat nearly always contains cheese or egg. Better restaurants, particularly in Málaga city, will be happy to prepare something, but otherwise stick to very simple dishes.

On the menu

Typical starters include *gazpacho* (a cold summer tomato soup flavoured with garlic, olive oil and peppers; *salmorejo* is a thicker version from Córdoba), *ensalada mixta* (mixed salad based on lettuce, tomatoes, tuna and more), or paella.

Main courses will usually be either meat or fish and are rarely served with any accompaniment beyond chips. Beef is common; the better steaks such as *solomillo* or *entrecot* are usually superbly tender. Spaniards tend to eat them fairly rare (*poco hecho*; ask for *al punto* for medium rare or *bien hecho* for well done). Pork is also widespread; *solomillo de cerdo*, *secreto*, *pluma* and *lomo* are all tasty cuts. Innards are popular: *callos* (tripe), *mollejas* (sweetbreads) and *morcilla* (black pudding) are excellent, if acquired, tastes.

Seafood is the pride of Andalucía. The region is famous for its *pescaíto frito* (fried fish) which typically consists of small fry such as whitebait in batter. Shellfish include *mejillones* (mussels), *gambas* (prawns) and *coquillas* (cockles). *Calamares* (calamari), *sepia* or *choco* (cuttlefish) and *chipirones* (small squid) are common, and you'll sometimes see *pulpo* (octopus). Among the vertebrates, *sardinas* (sardines), *dorada* (gilthead bream), *rape* (monkfish) and *pez espada* (swordfish) are all usually excellent. In the Alpujarra and other hilly areas you can enjoy freshwater *trucha* (trout).

Signature tapas dishes vary from bar to bar and from province to province, and part of the delight of Andalucía comes trying regional specialities. Ubiquitous are *jamón* (cured ham; the best, *ibérico*, comes from black-footed acorn-eating porkers that roam the woods of Huelva province and Extremadura) and *queso* (in Andalucía, usually the hard salty *manchego* from Castilla-la Mancha). *Gambas* (prawns) are usually on the tapas list; the best and priciest are from Huelva.

Desserts focus on the sweet and milky. *Flan* (a sort of crème caramel) is ubiquitous; great when *casero* (home-made), but often out of a plastic tub. *Natillas* are a similar but more liquid version, while Moorish-style pastries are also specialities of some areas.

Drink

Alcoholic drinks

In good Catholic fashion, wine is the blood of Spain. It's the standard accompaniment to meals, but also features prominently in bars. *Tinto* is red (if you just order *vino* this is what you'll get), *blanco* is white and rosé is *rosado*.

A well-regulated system of *denominaciones de origen* (DO), similar to the French *appellation d'origine contrôlée*, has lifted the quality and reputation of Spanish wines. While the daddy in terms of production and popularity is still Rioja, regions such as the Ribera del Duero, Rueda, Bierzo, Jumilla, Priorat and Valdepeñas have achieved worldwide recognition. The words *crianza*, *reserva* and *gran reserva* refer to the length and nature of the ageing process.

One of the joys of Spain, though, is the rest of the wine. Order a *menú del día* at a cheap restaurant and you'll be unceremoniously served a cheap bottle of local red. Wine snobbery can leave by the back door at this point: it may be cold, but you'll find it refreshing; it may be acidic, but once the olive-oil laden food arrives, you'll be glad of it. People add water to it if they feel like it, or *gaseosa* (lemonade) or cola (for the party drink *calimocho*).

Andalucía produces several table wines of this sort. The whites of the Condado region in eastern Huelva province and those from nearby Cádiz are simple seafood companions. Jaén province also has red grapes tucked between its seas of olive trees, mainly around Torreperogil near Ubeda. Bartenders throughout Andalucía tend to assume that tourists only want Rioja, so be sure to specify *vino corriente* (or *vino de la zona*) if you want to try the local stuff. As a general rule, only bars that serve food serve wine; most *pubs* and *discotecas* won't have it. Cheaper red wine is often served cold, a refreshing alternative in summer. *Tinto de verano* is a summery mix of red wine and lemonade, often with fruit added, while the stronger *sangría* adds healthy measures of sherry and sometimes spirits to the mix. The real vinous fame of the region comes, of course, from its fortified wines; sherries and others.

Beer is mostly lager, usually reasonably strong, fairly gassy, cold and good. Sweetish Cruzcampo from Sevilla is found throughout the region; other local brews include San Miguel, named after the archangel and brewed in Málaga, and Alhambra from Granada. A *caña* or *tubo* is a glass of draught beer, while just specifying *cerveza* usually gets you a bottle, otherwise known as a *botellín*. Many people order their beer *con gas* (half beer and half fizzy sweet water) or *con limón* (half lemonade, also called a *clara*).

Vermut (vermouth) is a popular pre-lunch aperitif. Many bars make their own vermouth by adding various herbs and fruits and letting it sit in barrels.

After dinner it's time for a *copa*. People relax over a whisky or a brandy, or hit the *cubatas* (mixed drinks); gin and tonic, rum and coke, whisky and coke are the most popular. Spirits are free-poured and large.

When ordering a spirit, you'll be expected to choose which brand you want; the range of, particularly, gins, is extraordinary. There's always a good selection of rum (*ron*) and blended whisky available too. *Chupitos* are short drinks often served in shot-glasses.

Non-alcoholic drinks

Zumo (fruit juice) is normally bottled; *mosto* (grape juice, really pre-fermented wine) is a popular soft drink in bars. All bars serve alcohol-free beer (*cerveza sin alcohol*). *Horchata* is a summer drink, a sort of milkshake made from tiger nuts. *Agua* (water) comes *con* (with) or *sin* (without) *gas*. The tap water is totally safe.

Café (coffee) is excellent and strong. *Solo* is black, served espresso style. Order *americano* if you want a long black, *cortado* if you want a dash of milk, or *con leche* for about half milk. *Té* (tea) is served without milk unless you ask; herbal teas (*infusiones*) are common, especially chamomile (*manzanilla*; don't confuse with the sherry of the same name) and mint (*menta poleo*).

Essentials A-Z

Accidents and emergencies

General emergencies 112.

Customs and duty free

Non-EU citizens are allowed to import 1 litre of spirits, 2 litres of wine and 200 cigarettes or 250 g of tobacco or 50 cigars. EU citizens are theoretically limited by personal use only.

Disabled travellers

Spain isn't the best equipped of countries in terms of disabled travel, but things are improving rapidly. By law, all new public buildings have to have full disabled access and facilities, but disabled toilets are rare elsewhere. Facilities generally are significantly better in Andalucía than in the rest of the country.

Most trains and stations are wheelchair friendly to some degree, as are many urban buses, but intercity buses are largely not accessible. **Hertz** in Málaga have a small range of cars set up with hand controls, but be sure to book them well in advance. Nearly all underground and municipal car parks have lifts and disabled spaces, as do many museums, castles, etc.

An invaluable resource for finding a bed are the regional accommodation lists, available from tourist offices and the www.andalucia.org website. Most of these include a disabled-access criterion. Many *hostales* are in buildings with ramps and lifts, but there are many that are not, and the lifts can be very small. Nearly all paradores and chain hotels are fully accessible by wheelchair, as is any accommodation built since 1995, but it's best to phone. Be sure to check details as many hotels' claims are well intentioned but not fully thought through.

While major cities are relatively straightforward, smaller towns and villages frequently have uneven footpaths, steep streets (often cobbled) and little, if any, disabled infrastructure.

Useful contacts
Confederación Nacional de Sordos de España (CNSE), www.cnse.es, has links to local associations for the deaf.
Global Access, www.globalaccessnews. com, has regular reports from disabled travellers as well as links to other sites.
Mobility Abroad, T0871-277 0888 (UK) or T+34-952 447764 (Spain), www. mobilityabroad.com, is a Málaga-based organization that provides support and hire of wheelchairs and disabled vehicles throughout the Costa del Sol area.
ONCE, www.once.es. The blind are well catered for as a result of the efforts of ONCE, the national organization for the blind, which runs a lucrative daily lottery. It can provide information on accessible attractions for blind travellers.

Electricity

230V. A round 2-pin plug is used (European standard).

Embassies and consulates

For a list of Spanish embassies abroad, see http://embassy.goabroad.com.

Festivals and public holidays

Festivals

Even the smallest village in Andalucía has a fiesta and many have several. Although mostly nominally religious featuring a mass and procession or two, they also offer live music, bullfights, competitions and fireworks. A feature of many are *gigantes y cabezudos*, huge-headed papier mâché figures based on historical personages who parade the streets. In many Andalucían villages there's a *Moros y Cristianos* festival, which recreates a Reconquista battle with colourful costumes. Most fiestas are in summer; expect some trouble finding accommodation. Details of the major town fiestas can be found in the travel text. National holidays and *puentes* (long weekends) can be difficult times to travel; it's important to reserve tickets in advance.

Public holidays

1 Jan **Año Nuevo**, New Year's Day.
6 Jan **Reyes Magos/Epifanía**, Epiphany, when Christmas presents are given.
28 Feb **Andalucía day**.
Easter **Jueves Santo, Viernes Santo, Día de Pascua** (Maundy Thu, Good Fri, Easter Sun).
1 May **Fiesta del Trabajo** (Labour Day).
24 Jun **Fiesta de San Juan** (Feast of St John and name-day of the king Juan Carlos I).
25 Jul **Día del Apostol Santiago**, Feast of St James.
15 Aug **Asunción**, Feast of the Assumption.
12 Oct **Día de la Hispanidad**, Spanish National Day (Columbus Day, Feast of the Virgin of the Pillar).
1 Nov **Todos los Santos**, All Saints' Day.
6 Dec **El Día de la Constitución Española**, Constitution Day.
8 Dec **Inmaculada Concepción**, Feast of the Immaculate Conception.
25 Dec **Navidad**, Christmas Day.

Gay and lesbian travellers

Homosexuality is legal, as is gay marriage, though it's just the sort of thing the incumbent Partido Popular would like to revoke. There are different levels of tolerance and open-mindedness towards gays and lesbians in Andalucía. In the larger cities and on the coast (particularly in summer), there's a substantial amount of gay life, although not on a par with Barcelona or Madrid. Inland, however, it can be a different story, and a couple walking hand-in-hand will likely be greeted with incredulous stares, although rarely anything worse. The most active scenes can be found in Torremolinos and Marbella.

Useful contacts

COLEGA, www.colegaweb.org. A gay and lesbian association with offices in many cities.
Shangay/Shanguide, www.shangay. com, is a useful magazine with reviews, events, information and city-by-city listings for the whole country.

Useful websites

www.damron.com Subscription listings and travel info.

Health

Medical facilities in Andalucía are very good. However, EU citizens should make sure they have the **European Health Insurance Card** (EHIC) to prove reciprocal rights to medical care. These are available free of charge in the UK from the Department of Health (www. dh.gov.uk) or post offices.

Non-EU citizens should consider travel insurance to cover emergency and routine medical needs; be sure that it covers any sports or activities you may do. Check for reciprocal cover with your private or public health scheme first.

Water is safe to drink. The **sun** in southern Spain can be harsh, so take precautions to avoid heat exhaustion and sunburn.

Many medications that require a prescription in other countries are available over the counter at pharmacies in Spain. Pharmacists are highly trained and usually speak some English. In medium-sized towns and cities, at least one pharmacy is open 24 hrs; this is performed on a rota system (posted in the window of all pharmacies and listed in local newspapers).

No vaccinations are needed.

Insurance

Insurance is a good idea to cover you for theft. In the unlucky event of theft, you'll have to make a report at the local police station within 24 hrs and obtain a *denuncia* (report) to show your insurers. See above for health cover for EU citizens.

Internet

Cyber cafés are increasingly rare in Spain, though you'll still find them in large cities. Other places that often offer access are *locutorios* (call shops), which are common in areas with a high immigrant population. Most accommodation and an increasing number of cafés and restaurants offer Wi-Fi. Internet places tend to appear and disappear rapidly, so we have minimized listings in this guide; ask the tourist information office for the latest place to get online. Mobile phone providers offer pay-as-you-go data SIM cards and USB modems at a reasonable rate. Roaming charges within the EU are set to be abolished in late 2015, so mobile data usage will cost EU residents no more in Andalucía than it would in your home country.

Language

Everyone in Andalucía – except many of the large expat population – speaks Spanish, known either as *castellano* or *español*, and it's a huge help to know some. The local accent, *andaluz*, is characterized by dropping consonants left, right and centre, thus *dos tapas* tends to be pronounced *dotapa*. Unlike in the rest of Spain, the letters 'c' and 'z' in words such as *cerveza* aren't pronounced 'th' (although in Cádiz province, perversely, they tend to pronounce 's' with that sound).

Most young people know some English, and standards are rising fast, but don't assume that people aged 40 or over know any at all. Spaniards are often shy to attempt to speak English. On the coast, high numbers of expats and tourists mean that bartenders and shopkeepers know some English. While many visitor attractions have some sort of information available in English (and to a lesser extent French and German), many don't, or have English tours only in times of high demand. Most tourist office staff will speak at least some English and there's a good range of translated information available in most places. People are used to speaking English in well-visited areas, but trying even a couple of words of Spanish is basic politeness. Small courtesies grease the wheels of everyday interaction here:

greet the proprietor or waiting staff when entering a shop or bar, and say *hasta luego* when leaving. See page 120, for useful words and phrases in Spanish.

Language schools
Amerispan, www.amerispan.com. Immersion programmes in Málaga.
Instituto Picasso, Pl de la Merced 20, Málaga, T952-213932, www.instituto-picasso.com.
Languages Abroad, www.languagesabroad.com. Immersion courses in Málaga.
Spanish Abroad, www.spanishabroad.com. 2-week immersion language courses in Málaga and Marbella.

Money

Currency and exchange
For up-to-the-minute exchange rates visit www.xe.com.

In 2002, Spain switched to the euro, bidding farewell to the peseta. The euro (€) is divided into 100 *céntimos*. Euro notes are standard across the whole euro zone and come in denominations of 5, 10, 20, 50, 100, and the rarely seen 200 and 500. Coins have one standard face and one national face; all coins are, however, acceptable in all countries. The coins are slightly difficult to tell apart when you're not used to them. The coppers are 1, 2 and 5 cent pieces, the golds are 10, 20 and 50, and the silver/gold combinations are €1 and €2. The exchange rate was approximately €6 to 1000 pesetas or 166 pesetas to the euro. Some people still quote large amounts, like house prices, in pesetas.

ATMs and banks
The best way to get money in Spain is by plastic. ATMs are plentiful and accept all the major international debit and credit cards. The Spanish bank won't charge for the transaction, though they will charge a mark-up on the exchange rate, but beware of your own bank hitting you for a hefty fee: check with them before leaving home. Even if they do, it's likely to be a better deal than changing cash over a counter.

Banks are usually open Mon-Fri (and Sat in winter) 0830-1430 and many change foreign money (sometimes only the central branch in a town will do it). Commission rates vary widely; it's usually best to change large amounts, as there's often a minimum commission. The website www.moneysavingexpert.com has a good rundown on the most economical ways of accessing cash while travelling.

Cost of living
Prices have soared since the euro was introduced; some basics rose by 50-80% in 3 years, and hotel and restaurant prices can even seem dear by Western European standards these days. Nevertheless, Málaga still offers value for money, and you can get by cheaply if you forgo a few luxuries. If you're travelling as a pair, staying in cheap *pensiones*, eating a set meal at lunchtime, travelling short distances by bus or train daily, and snacking on tapas in the evenings, €65 per person per day is reasonable. If you camp and grab picnic lunches from shops, you could reduce this somewhat. In a good *hostal* or cheap hotel and using a car, €150 a day and you'll not be counting pennies; €300 per day and you'll be very comfy indeed unless you're staying in 5-star accommodation.

Accommodation is usually more expensive in summer than winter, particularly on the coast, where hotels and *hostales* in seaside towns are overpriced.

Public transport is generally cheap; intercity bus services are quick and low-priced, though the new fast trains are expensive. If you're hiring a car, Málaga is the cheapest place in Andalucía. Standard unleaded petrol is around 150 cents per litre. In some places, particularly in tourist areas, you may be charged up to 20% more to sit outside a restaurant. It's also worth checking if the 10% IVA (sales tax) is included in menu prices, especially in the more expensive restaurants; it should say on the menu.

Opening hours

Business hours Mon-Fri 1000-1400, 1700-2000; Sat 1000-1400. **Banks** Mon-Fri, plus sometimes Sat in winter, 0830-1430. **Government offices** Mornings only.

Post

The Spanish post is still notoriously inefficient and slow by European standards. *Correos* (post offices) generally open Mon-Fri 0800-1300, 1700-2000; Sat 0800-1300, although main offices in large towns will stay open all day. Stamps can be bought here or at *estancos* (tobacconists).

Safety

Málaga is a very safe place to travel. There's been a crackdown on tourist crime in recent years and even large cities like Málaga feel much safer than their equivalents in, say, England.

What tourist crime there is tends to be of the opportunistic kind. Robberies from parked cars (particularly those with foreign plates) or snatch-and-run thefts from vehicles stopped at traffic lights are not unknown, and the occasional mugger operates in Málaga city. Keep car doors locked when driving. If parking in a city or a popular hiking zone, make it clear there's nothing worth robbing in a car by opening the glove compartment.

If you are unfortunate enough to be robbed, you should report the theft immediately at the nearest police station, as insurance companies will require a copy of the *denuncia* (police report).

Smoking

Smoking is widespread in Spain, but it's been banned in all enclosed public spaces (ie bars and restaurants) since 2011. There are still rooms for smokers in some hotels, but these are limited to 30% of the total rooms. Prices are standardized; you can buy cigarettes at tobacconists or at machines in cafés and bars (with a small surcharge).

Student travellers

An **International Student Identity Card** (ISIC; www.isic.org), for full-time students, is worth having in Spain. Get one at your place of study, or at many travel agencies both in and outside Spain. The cost varies from country to country, but is generally about €6-10 – a good investment, providing discounts of up to 20% on some plane fares, train tickets, museum entries, bus tickets and some accommodation. A **European Youth Card** (www.eyca.org) card gives similar discounts for anyone under 30 years of age.

Taxes

Nearly all goods and services in Spain are subject to a value-added tax (IVA). This is 10% for things like supermarket supplies, hotels and restaurant meals, but is 21% on luxury goods such as computer equipment. IVA is normally included in the stated prices. You're technically entitled to claim it back if you're a non-EU citizen, for purchases over €90. If you're buying something pricey, make sure you get a stamped receipt clearly showing the IVA component, as well as your name and passport number; you can claim the amount back at major airports on departure. Some shops will have a form to smooth the process.

Telephone

Country code +34; **IDD Code** 00
Phone booths on the street are dwindling. Those that remain are mostly operated by **Telefónica**, and all have international direct dialling. They accept coins from €0.05 upwards and phone cards, which can be bought from *kioscos* (newspaper kiosks).

Domestic landlines have 9-digit numbers beginning with 9. Although the first 3 digits indicate the province, you have to dial the full number from wherever you are calling, including abroad. Mobile numbers start with 6.

Most foreign mobiles will work in Spain (although older North American ones won't); check with your service provider about what the call costs will be like. Roaming charges within the EU are set to be abolished from late 2015. Many mobile networks require you to call before leaving your home country to activate overseas service (roaming). If you're staying a while and have an unlocked phone, it's pretty cheap to buy a Spanish SIM card.

Time

1 hr ahead of GMT. Clocks go forward an hour in late Mar and back in late Oct with the rest of the EU.

Tipping

Tipping in Spain is far from compulsory. A 10% tip would be considered extremely generous in a restaurant; 3% to 5% is more usual. It's rare for a service charge to be added to a bill. Waiters don't expect tips but in bars and cafés people will sometimes leave small change, especially for table service. Taxi drivers don't expect a tip, but will be pleased to receive one.

Tourist information

The tourist information infrastructure in Andalucía is organized by the Junta (the regional government) and is generally excellent, with a wide range of information, often in English, German and French as well as Spanish. The website www.andalucia.org has comprehensive information and *Oficinas de turismo* (local government tourist offices) are in all the major towns, providing more specific local information. In addition, many towns run a municipal *turismo*, offering locally produced material. The tourist offices are generally open during normal office hours and in the main holiday areas normally have enthusiastic, multilingual staff. The tourist offices can provide local maps and town plans and a full list of registered accommodation. Staff are not allowed to make recommendations. If you're in a car, it's especially worth asking for a listing of *casas rurales* (rural accommodation). In villages with no *turismo* you could try asking for local information on accommodation and sights in the *ayuntamiento* (town hall). Some city tourist offices offer downloadable smartphone content.

There is a substantial amount of tourist information on the internet. Apart from the websites listed (see below), many towns and villages have their own site with information on sights, hotels and restaurants, although this may be in Spanish.

The **Spanish Tourist Board** (www. spain.info) produces a mass of information that you can obtain before you leave from their offices located in many countries abroad.

Useful websites

www.alsa.es One of the country's main bus companies with online booking.

www.andalucia.com Excellent site with comprehensive practical and background information on Andalucía, covering everything from accommodation to zoos.

www.andalucia.org The official tourist-board site, with details of even the smallest villages, accommodation and tourist offices.

www.booking.com The most useful online accommodation booker for Spain.

www.dgt.es The transport department website has up-to-date information in Spanish on road conditions throughout the country.

www.elpais.com Online edition of Spain's biggest-selling daily paper. Also in English.

www.guiarepsol.com Online route planner for Spanish roads, also available in English.

www.inm.es Site of the national metereological institute, with the day's weather and next-day forecasts.

www.inturjoven.com Details of youth hostel locations, facilities and prices.

maps.google.es Street maps of most Spanish towns and cities.

www.movelia.es Online timetables and ticketing for some bus companies.

www.paginasamarillas.es Yellow Pages.

www.paginasblancas.es White Pages.

www.parador.es Parador information, including locations, prices and photos.

www.raar.es Andalucían rural accommodation network with details of mainly self-catering accommodation to rent, including cottages and farmhouses.

www.renfe.com Online timetables and tickets for RENFE train network.

www.spain.info The official website of the Spanish tourist board.

www.soccer-spain.com A website in English dedicated to Spanish football.

www.surinenglish.com The weekly English edition of the Málaga *Sur* paper.

www.ticketmaster.es Spain's biggest ticketing agency for concerts and more, with online purchase.

www.toprural.com and **www.todo turismorural.com** 2 of many sites for *casas rurales*.

www.tourspain.es A useful website run by the Spanish tourist board.

www.typicallyspanish.com News and links on all things Spanish.

Tour operators

UK and Ireland

Exodus, www.exodus.co.uk. Walking and adventure tours to suit all pockets.

North America

Heritage Tours, www.htprivatetravel. com. Interesting, classy itineraries around the south of Spain.
Magical Spain, www.magicalspain.com. American-run tour agency based in Sevilla, who runs a variety of tours.
Spain Adventures, www.spain adventures.com. Organizes a range of hiking and biking tours, including Ronda.

Australia

Ibertours,www.ibertours.com.au. Spanish specialist and booking agent for **Parador** and **Rusticae** hotels.
Timeless Tours & Travel, www.timeless. com.au. Specializes in tailored itineraries for Spain.

Visas and immigration

EU citizens and those from countries within the Schengen agreement can enter Spain freely. UK and Irish citizens will need to carry a passport, while an identity card suffices for other EU/ Schengen nationals. Citizens of Australia, the USA, Canada, New Zealand, several Latin American countries and Israel can enter without a visa for up to 90 days. Other citizens will require a visa, obtainable from Spanish consulates or embassies. These are usually issued quickly and are valid for all Schengen countries. The basic visa is valid for 90 days, and you'll need 2 passport photos, proof of funds covering your stay, and possibly evidence of medical cover (ie insurance).

For extensions of visas, apply to an *oficina de extranjeros* in a major city (usually in the *comisaría*, main police station).

Weights and measures

Metric.

Working in the country

The most obvious paid work for English speakers is through teaching the language. Even the smallest towns usually have an English college or two. Rates of pay aren't great except in the large cities, but you can live quite comfortably. The best way of finding work is by trawling around the schools, but there are dozens of useful internet sites; check www.eslcafe.com for links and listings. There's also a more casual scene of private teaching; noticeboards in universities and student cafés are the best way to find work of this sort, or to advertise your own services. Standard rates for 1-to-1 classes are €15-30 per hr.

Bar work is also relatively easy to find, particularly in summer on the coast. Live-in English-speaking au pairs and childminders are also popular with wealthier city families. The **International Au Pair Association** (www.iapa.org) lists reliable agencies that arrange placements. The online forum **Au Pair World** (www.aupairworld.net) is a popular free service.

EU citizens are at an advantage when it comes to working in Spain; they can work without a permit. Non-EU citizens need a working visa, obtainable from Spanish embassies or consulates, but you'll need to have a firm offer of work to obtain it. Most English schools can organize this for you but make sure you arrange it before arriving in the country.

Another popular line of work for travellers is crewing on yachts; the best places to pick up work of this sort are Marbella/Puerto Banús.

Basic Spanish

Learning Spanish is a useful part of the preparation for a trip to Spain and no volumes of dictionaries, phrase books or word lists will provide the same enjoyment as being able to communicate directly with the people of the country you are visiting. It is a good idea to make an effort to grasp the basics before you go. As you travel you will pick up more of the language and the more you know, the more you will benefit from your stay. Regional accents and usages vary, but the basic language is essentially the same everywhere.

Vowels

a	as in English *cat*
e	as in English *best*
i	as the ee in English *feet*
o	as in English *shop*
u	as the oo in English *food*
ai	as the i in English *ride*
ei	as ey in English *they*
oi	as oy in English *toy*

Consonants

Most consonants can be pronounced more or less as they are in English. The exceptions are:

g	before *e* or *i* is the same as *j*
h	is always silent (except in *ch* as in *chair*)
j	as the *ch* in Scottish *loch*
ll	as the *y* in *yellow*
ñ	as the *ni* in English *onion*
rr	trilled much more than in English
x	depending on its location, pronounced *x*, *s*, *sh* or *j*

Spanish words and phrases

Greetings, courtesies

hello	*hola*	thank you (very much)	*(muchas) gracias*
good morning	*buenos días*		
good afternoon/evening	*buenas tardes/ noches*	I speak a little Spanish	*hablo un poco de español*
goodbye	*adiós/ hasta luego*	I don't speak Spanish	*no hablo español*
		do you speak English?	*¿hablas inglés?*
pleased to meet you	*encantado/a*	I don't understand	*no entiendo*
how are you?	*¿cómo estás?*	please speak slowly	*habla despacio por favor*
I'm called ...	*me llamo ...*		
what is your name?	*¿cómo te llamas?*	I am very sorry	*lo siento mucho/ discúlpame*
I'm fine, thanks	*muy bien, gracias*	what do you want?	*¿qué quieres?*
		I want/would like	*quiero/quería*
yes/no	*sí/no*	I don't want it	*no lo quiero*
please	*por favor*	good/bad	*bueno/malo*

Basic questions and requests

have you got a room for two people?
¿tienes una habitación para dos personas?

how do I get to_? *¿cómo llego a_?*

how much does it cost?
¿cuánto cuesta? ¿cuánto es?

is VAT included? *¿el IVA está incluido?*

when does the bus leave (arrive)?
¿a qué hora sale (llega) el autobús?

when? *¿cuándo?*

where is_? *¿dónde está_?*

where can I buy? *¿dónde puedo comprar...?*

where is the nearest petrol station?
¿dónde está la gasolinera más cercana?

why? *¿por qué?*

Basic words and phrases

bank	*el banco*	market	*el mercado*
bathroom/toilet	*el baño*	note/coin	*el billete/la moneda*
to be	*ser, estar*	police (policeman)	*la policía (el policía)*
bill	*la factura/la cuenta*	post office	*el correo*
cash	*efectivo*	public telephone	*el teléfono público*
cheap	*barato/a*	shop	*la tienda*
credit card	*la tarjeta de crédito*	supermarket	*el supermercado*
exchange rate	*el tipo de cambio*	there is/are	*hay*
expensive	*caro/a*	there isn't/aren't	*no hay*
to go	*ir*	ticket office	*la taquilla*
to have	*tener, haber*	traveller's cheques	*los cheques de viaje*

Getting around

aeroplane	*el avión*	luggage	*el equipaje*
airport	*el aeropuerto*	motorway, freeway	*el autopista/autovía*
arrival/departure	*la llegada/salida*	north/south/	*el norte, el sur,*
avenue	*la avenida*	west/east	*el oeste, el este*
border	*la frontera*	oil	*el aceite*
bus station	*la estación de autobuses*	to park	*aparcar*
		passport	*el pasaporte*
bus	*el bus/el autobús/ el camión*	petrol/gasoline	*la gasolina*
		puncture	*el pinchazo*
corner	*la esquina*	street	*la calle*
customs	*la aduana*	that way	*por allí*
left/right	*izquierda/derecha*	this way	*por aquí*
ticket	*el billete*	tyre	*el neumático*
empty/full	*vacío/lleno*	unleaded	*sin plomo*
highway, main road	*la carretera*	waiting room	*la sala de espera*
insurance	*el seguro*	to walk	*caminar/andar*
insured person	*el asegurado/la asegurada*		

Accommodation

air conditioning	*el aire acondicionado*	restaurant	*el restaurante*
all-inclusive	*todo incluido*	room/bedroom	*la habitación*
bathroom, private	*el baño privado*	sheets	*las sábanas*
bed, double	*la cama matrimonial*	shower	*la ducha*
		soap	*el jabón*
blankets	*las mantas*	toilet	*el inódoro*
to clean	*limpiar*	toilet paper	*el papel higiénico*
dining room	*el comedor*	towels, clean/dirty	*las toallas limpias sucias*
hotel	*el hotel*		
noisy	*ruidoso*	water, hot/cold	*el agua caliente/ fría*
pillows	*las almohadas*		

Health

aspirin	*la aspirina*	diarrhoea	*la diarrea*
blood	*la sangre*	doctor	*el médico*
chemist	*la farmacia*	fever/sweat	*la fiebre/el sudor*
condoms	*los preservativos, los condones*	pain	*el dolor*
		head	*la cabeza*
contact lenses	*los lentes de contacto*	period	*la regla*
		sanitary towels	*las toallas femininas*
contraceptives	*los anticonceptivos*	stomach	*el estómago*
contraceptive pill	*la píldora anticonceptiva*		

Family

family	*la familia*	boyfriend/girlfriend	*el novio/la novia*
brother/sister	*el hermano/ la hermana*	friend	*el amigo/ la amiga*
daughter/son	*la hija/el hijo*	married	*casado/a*
father/mother	*el padre/la madre*	single/unmarried	*soltero/a*
husband/wife	*el esposo (marido)/la mujer*		

Months, days and time

January	*enero*	July	*julio*
February	*febrero*	August	*agosto*
March	*marzo*	September	*septiembre*
April	*abril*	October	*octubre*
May	*mayo*	November	*noviembre*
June	*junio*	December	*diciembre*

Monday	*lunes*	it's one o'clock	*es la una*
Tuesday	*martes*	it's seven o'clock	*son las siete*
Wednesday	*miércoles*	it's six twenty	*son las seis y veinte*
Thursday	*jueves*		
Friday	*viernes*	it's five to nine	*son las nueve menos cinco*
Saturday	*sábado*		
Sunday	*domingo*	in ten minutes	*en diez minutos*
at one o'clock	*a la una*	five hours	*cinco horas*
at half past two	*a las dos y media*	does it take long?	*¿tarda mucho?*
at a quarter to three	*a las tres menos cuarto*		

Numbers

one	*uno*	sixteen	*dieciséis*
two	*dos*	seventeen	*diecisiete*
three	*tres*	eighteen	*dieciocho*
four	*cuatro*	nineteen	*diecinueve*
five	*cinco*	twenty	*veinte*
six	*seis*	twenty-one	*veintiuno*
seven	*siete*	thirty	*treinta*
eight	*ocho*	forty	*cuarenta*
nine	*nueve*	fifty	*cincuenta*
ten	*diez*	sixty	*sesenta*
eleven	*once*	seventy	*setenta*
twelve	*doce*	eighty	*ochenta*
thirteen	*trece*	ninety	*noventa*
fourteen	*catorce*	hundred	*cien/ciento*
fifteen	*quince*	thousand	*mil*

Food glossary

A

acedía	small wedge sole
aceite	oil; *aceite de oliva* is olive oil and *aceite de girasol* is sunflower oil
aceitunas	olives, also sometimes called *olivas*. The best kind are unripe green *manzanilla*, particularly when stuffed with anchovy, *rellenas con anchoas*
adobo	marinated fried nuggets usually of shark (*tiburón*) or dogfish (*cazón*); delicious
agua	water
aguacate	avocado
ahumado	smoked; *tabla de ahumados* is a mixed plate of smoked fish
ajillo (al)	cooked in garlic, most commonly *gambas* or *pollo*
ajo	garlic, *ajetes* are young garlic shoots, often in a *revuelto*
ajo arriero	a simple sauce of garlic, paprika and parsley
ajo blanco	a chilled garlic and almond soup, a speciality of Málaga
albóndigas	meatballs
alcachofa/ alcaucil	artichoke
alcaparras	capers
aliño	any salad marinated in vinegar, olive oil and salt; often made with egg or potato, with chopped onion, peppers and tomato

alioli	a tasty sauce made from raw garlic blended with oil and egg yolk; also called *ajoaceite*
almejas	name applied to various species of small clams, often cooked with garlic, parsley and white wine
almendra	almond
alubias	broad beans
anchoa	preserved anchovy
anchoba/ anjova	bluefish
añejo	aged (of cheeses, rums, etc)
angulas	baby eels, a delicacy that has become scarce and expensive. Far more common are *gulas*, false *angulas* made from putting processed fish through a spaghetti machine; squid ink is used for authentic colouring
anís	aniseed, commonly used to flavour biscuits and liqueurs
arroz	rice; *arroz con leche* is a sweet rice pudding
asado	roast. An *asador* is a restaurant specializing in charcoal-roasted meat and fish
atún	blue-fin tuna
azúcar	sugar

B

bacalao	salted cod, either superb or leathery
berberechos	cockles
berenjena	aubergine/eggplant
besugo	red bream
bistec	steak. *Poco hecho* is rare, *al punto* is medium rare, *regular* is medium, *muy hecho* is well done
bizcocho	sponge cake or biscuit
bocadillo/ bocata	a crusty filled roll
bogavante	lobster
bonito	atlantic bonito, a small tuna fish
boquerones	fresh anchovies, often served filleted in garlic and oil
botella	bottle
(a la) brasa	cooked on a griddle over coals
buey	ox

C

caballa	mackerel
cacahuetes	peanuts
café	coffee; *solo* is black, served espresso-style; *cortado* adds a dash of milk, *con leche* more; *americano* is a long black coffee
calamares	squid
caldereta	a stew of meat or fish usually made with sherry; *venao* (venison) is commonly used, and delicious
caldo	a thin soup
callos	tripe
caña	a glass of draught beer
cangrejo	crab; occasionally river crayfish
caracol	snail; very popular in Sevilla *cabrillas*, *burgaos*, and *blanquillos* are popular varieties
caramelos	boiled sweets
carne	meat
carta	menu
casero	home-made
castañas	chestnuts
cava	sparkling wine, mostly produced in Catalunya
cazuela	a stew, often of fish or seafood
cebolla	onion
cena	dinner
centollo	spider crab
cerdo	pork
cerezas	cherries
cerveza	beer
champiñón	mushroom
chipirones	small squid, often served *en su tinta*, in its own ink, mixed with butter and garlic
chocolate	a popular afternoon drink; also slang for hashish
choco	cuttlefish
chorizo	a red sausage, versatile and of varying spiciness (*picante*)
choto	roast kid
chuleta/ chuletilla	chop
chuletón	a massive T-bone steak, often sold by weight
churrasco	barbecued meat, often ribs with a spicy sauce
churro	a fried dough-stick usually eaten with hot chocolate (*chocolate con churros*). Usually eaten as a late afternoon snack (*merienda*), but sometimes for breakfast

cigala	Dublin Bay prawn/Norway lobster
ciruela	plum
cochinillo	suckling pig
cocido	a heavy stew, usually of meat and chickpeas/beans; *sopa de cocido* is the broth
codorniz	quail
cogollo	lettuce heart
comida	lunch
conejo	rabbit
congrio	conger eel
cordero	lamb
costillas	ribs
crema catalana	a lemony crème brûlée
criadillas	hog or bull testicles
croquetas	deep-fried crumbed balls of meat, béchamel, seafood, or vegetables
cuchara	spoon
cuchillo	knife
cuenta (la)	the bill

D

desayuno	breakfast
dorada	a species of bream (gilthead)
dulce	sweet

E

ecológico	organic
embutido	any salami-type sausage
empanada	a pie, pasty-like (*empanadilla*) or in large flat tins and sold by the slice; *atun* or *bonito* is a common filling, as is ham, mince or seafood
ensalada	salad; *mixta* is usually a large serve of a bit of everything; excellent option

ensaladilla rusa	Russian salad, with potato, peas and carrots in mayonnaise
escabeche	pickled in wine and vinegar
espárragos	asparagus, white and usually canned
espinacas	spinach
estofado	braised, often in stew form

F

fabada	the most famous of Asturian dishes, a hearty stew of beans, *chorizo*, and *morcilla*
fideuá	a bit like a paella but with noodles
filete	steak
fino	the classic dry sherry
flamenquín	a fried and crumbed finger of meat stuffed with ham
flan	the ubiquitous crème caramel, great when home-made (*casero*), awful when it's not
foie	fattened goose liver; often made into a thick gravy sauce
frambuesas	raspberries
fresas	strawberries
frito/a	fried
fruta	fruit

G

galletas	biscuits
gallo	rooster, also the flatfish megrim
gambas	prawns
garbanzos	chickpeas, often served in *espinacas con garbanzos*, a spicy spinach dish that is a signature of Seville
gazpacho	a cold garlicky tomato soup, very refreshing

granizado	popular summer drink, like a frappé fruit milkshake
guisado/ guiso	stewed/a stew
guisantes	peas

H

habas	broad beans, often deliciously stewed *con jamón*, with ham
harina	flour
helado	ice cream
hígado	liver
higo	fig
hojaldre	puff pastry
horno (al)	oven (baked)
hueva	fish roe
huevo	egg

I/J

ibérico	see *jamón*; the term can also refer to other pork products
infusión	herbal tea
jabalí	wild boar
jamón	ham; *jamón York* is cooked British-style ham. Far better is cured *jamón serrano*; *ibérico* ham comes from Iberian pigs in western Spain fed on acorns (*bellotas*). Some places, like Jabugo, are famous for their hams, which can be expensive
judías verdes	green beans
jerez (al)	cooked in sherry

L

langosta	crayfish
langostinos	king prawns
lechazo	milk-fed lamb
leche	milk
lechuga	lettuce
lengua	tongue
lenguado	sole
lentejas	lentils
limón	lemon
lomo	loin, usually sliced pork, sometimes tuna
lubina	sea bass

M

macedonia de frutas	fruit salad, usually tinned
manchego	Spain's national cheese; hard, whitish and made from ewe's milk
manitas (de cerdo)	pork trotters
mantequilla	butter
manzana	apple
manzanilla	the dry, salty sherry from Sanlúcar de Barrameda; also, confusingly, camomile tea and the tastiest type of olive
marisco	shellfish
mejillones	mussels
melocotón	peach, usually canned and served in *almíbar* (syrup)
melva	frigate mackerel, often served tinned or semi-dried
menestra	a vegetable stew, usually served like a minestrone without the liquid; vegetarians will be annoyed to find that it's often seeded with ham and bits of pork
menú	a set meal, usually consisting of three or more courses, bread and wine or water

menudo	tripe stew, usually with chickpeas and mint	parrilla	grill; a *parrillada* is a mixed grill
merluza	hake is to Spain as rice is to southeast Asia	pastel	cake/pastry
mero	grouper	patatas	potatoes; often chips (*patatas fritas*, which confusingly can also refer to crisps); *bravas* are with a spicy tomato sauce
miel	honey		
migas	breadcrumbs, fried and often mixed with lard and meat to form a delicious rural dish of the same name		
		pato	duck
		pavía	a crumbed and fried nugget of fish, usually *bacalao* or *merluza*
Mojama	salt-cured tuna, most common in Cádiz province		
mollejas	sweetbreads; ie the pancreas of a calf or lamb	pavo	turkey
		pechuga	breast (usually chicken)
montadito	a small toasted filled roll	perdiz	partridge
morcilla	blood sausage, either solid or semi-liquid	pescado	fish
		pescaíto frito	Andalucían deep-fried fish and seafood
morro	cheek, pork or lamb	pestiños	an Arabic-style confection of pastry and honey, traditionally eaten during Semana Santa
mostaza	mustard		
mosto	grape juice. Can also refer to a young wine, from 3 months old		
		pez espada	swordfish; delicious; sometimes called *emperador*

N

naranja	orange		
nata	sweet whipped cream	picadillo	a dish of spicy mincemeat
natillas	rich custard dessert		
navajas	razor shells	picante	hot, ie spicy
nécora	small sea crab, sometimes called a velvet crab	pichón	squab
		pijota	whiting
nueces	walnuts	pimienta	pepper
		pimientos	peppers; there are many kinds, *piquillos* are the trademark thin Basque red pepper; Padrón produces sweet green mini ones. A popular tapa is *pimientos aliñados* (marinated roasted peppers, often with onion, sometimes with tuna)

O

orejas	ears, usually of a pig		
oruja	a fiery grape spirit, often brought to add to black coffee if the waiter likes you		
ostras	oysters, also a common expression of dismay		

P

paella	rice dish with saffron, seafood and/or meat
pan	bread

pincho	a small snack or grilled meat on a skewer (or *pinchito*)
pipas	sunflower seeds, a common snack
pisto	a ratatouille-like vegetable concoction
plancha (a la)	grilled on a hot iron or fried in a pan without oil
plátano	banana
pluma	a cut of pork next to the loin
pollo	chicken
postre	dessert
potaje	a soup or stew
pringá	a tasty paste of stewed meats usually eaten in a *montadito* and a traditional final tapa of the evening
puerros	leeks
pulpo	octopus, particularly delicious *a la gallega*, boiled Galician style and garnished with olive oil, salt and paprika
puntillitas	small squid, often served crumbed and deep fried

Q/R

queso	cheese; *de cabra* (goat's), *oveja* (sheep's) or *vaca* (cow's). It comes fresh (*fresco*), medium (*semicurado*) or strong (*curado*)
rabo de buey/toro	oxtail
ración	a portion of food served in cafés and bars; check the size and order a half (*media*) if you want less
rana	frog; *ancas de rana* is frogs' legs
rape	monkfish/anglerfish
raya	any of a variety of rays and skates
rebujito	a weak mix of *manzanilla* and lemonade, consumed by the bucketload during Andalucían festivals
relleno/a	stuffed
reserva, gran reserva, crianza	terms relating to the age of wines; *gran reserva* is the oldest and finest, then *reserva* followed by *crianza*
revuelto	scrambled eggs, usually with wild mushrooms (*setas*) or seafood; often a speciality
riñones	kidneys
rodaballo	turbot; pricey and delicious
romana (à la)	fried in batter
rosca	a large round dish, a cross between sandwich and pizza
rosquilla	doughnut

S

sal	salt
salchicha	sausage
salchichón	a salami-like sausage
salmón	salmon
salmonete	red mullet
salmorejo	a delicious thicker version of gazpacho, often garnished with egg and cured ham
salpicón	a seafood salad with plenty of onion and vinegar
salsa	sauce
San Jacobo	a steak cooked with ham and cheese
sandía	watermelon
sardinas	sardines, delicious grilled

sargo	white sea bream	tomate	tomato
seco	dry	torrijas	a Semana Santa dessert, bread fried in milk and covered in honey and cinnamon
secreto	a cut of pork loin		
sepia	cuttlefish		
serrano	see *jamón*		
setas	wild mushrooms, often superb	tortilla	a Spanish omelette, with potato, egg, olive oil and optional onion; *tortilla francesa* is a French omelette
sidra	cider		
solomillo	beef or pork steak cut from the sirloin bone, deliciously fried in whisky and garlic in Sevilla (*solomillo al whisky*)		
		tostada	toasted, also a toasted breakfast roll eaten with olive oil, tomato or pâté
sopa	soup; *sopa castellana* is a broth with a fried egg, noodles, and bits of ham	trucha	trout

U/V

		uva	grape
T		vaso	glass
tapa	a saucer-sized portion of bar food	venado/ venao	venison
tarta	tart or cake	verduras	vegetables
té	tea	vieiras	scallops, also called *veneras*
tenedor	fork	vino	wine; *blanco* is white, *rosado* or *clarete* is rosé, *tinto* is red
ternera	veal or young beef		
tinto	red wine is *vino tinto*; a *tinto de verano* is mixed with lemonade and ice, a refreshing option		
		Z	
		zanahoria	carrot
tocino	pork lard; *tocinillo de cielo* is a caramelized egg dessert	zumo	fruit juice, usually bottled and pricey

Glossary of architectural terms

A

alcázar a Moorish fort

ambulatory a gallery round the chancel and behind the altar

apse vaulted square or rounded recess at the back of a church

archivolt decorative carving around the outer surface of an arch

art deco a style that evolved between the World Wars, based on geometric forms

artesonado ceiling ceiling of carved wooden panels with Islamic motifs popular throughout Spain in the 15th and 16th centuries

ayuntamiento a town hall

azulejo an ornamental ceramic tile

B

Baldacchino an ornate carved canopy above an altar or tomb

Baroque ornate architectural style of the 17th and 18th centuries

bodega a cellar where wine is kept or made; the term also refers to modern wineries and wine shops

buttress a pillar built into a wall to reinforce areas of greatest stress. A flying buttress is set away from the wall; a feature of Gothic architecture

C

capilla a chapel within a church or cathedral

capital the top of column, joining it to another section. Often highly decorated

castillo a castle or fort

catedral a cathedral, ie the seat of a bishop

chancel the area of a church which contains the main altar, usually at the eastern end

chapterhouse area reserved for Bible study in monastery or church

Churrigueresque a particularly ornate form of Spanish Baroque, named after the Churriguera brothers

colegiata a collegiate church, ie one ruled by a chapter of canons

conjunto histórico a tourist-board term referring to an area of historic buildings

convento	a monastery or convent
coro	the area enclosing the choirstalls, often central and completely closed off in Spanish churches
crossing	the centre of a church, where the 'arms' of the cross join

E
ermita	a hermitage or rural chapel

G
Gothic	13th-15th-century style formerly known as pointed style; distinguished externally by pinnacles and tracery around windows, Gothic architecture lays stress on the presence of light

H
hospital	in pilgrimage terms, a place where pilgrims used to be able to rest, receive nourishment and receive medical attention

I
iglesia	a church

L
lobed arch	Moorish arch with depressions in the shape of simple arches
lonja	a guildhall or fish market

M
mocárabes	small concave spaces used as a decorative feature on Moorish ceilings and archways
modernista	a particularly imaginative variant of art nouveau that came out of Catalonia; exemplified by Gaudí
monasterio	a large monastery usually located in a rural area
monstrance	a ceremonial container for displaying the host
Mozarabic	the style of Christian artisans living under Moorish rule
mudéjar	the work of Muslims living under Christian rule after the Reconquest, characterized by ornate brickwork
multifoil	a type of Muslim-influenced arch with consecutive circular depressions
muralla	a city wall

N
nave	the main body of the church, a single or multiple passageway leading (usually) from the western end up to the crossing or high altar
neoclassical	a reaction against the excesses of Spanish Baroque, this 18th- and 19th-century style saw clean lines and symmetry valued above all things

P

palacio a palace or large residence

patio an interior courtyard

pediment triangular section between top of collums and gables

pilaster pillar attached to the wall

Plateresque derived from *platero* (silversmith); used to describe a Spanish Renaissance style characterized by finely carved decoration

R

reliquary a container to hold bones or remains of saints and other holy things

Renaissance Spanish Renaissance architecture began when classical motifs were used in combination with Gothic elements in the 16th century

retablo altarpiece or retable formed by many panels often rising to roof level; can be painted or sculptured

Romanesque (románico) style spread from France in the 11th and 12th centuries, characterized by barrel vaulting, rounded apses and semicircular arches

Romano Roman

S

sacristy (sacristía) part of church reserved for priests to prepare for services

soportales wooden or stone supports for the 1st floor of civic buildings, forming an arcade underneath

stucco (yesería) moulding mix consisting mainly of plaster; fundamental part of Moorish architecture

Index → Entries in **bold** refer to maps

FOOTPRINT

Features

Credits

Footprint credits

Editor: Jo Williams
Production and layout: Emma Bryers
Maps: Kevin Feeney
Colour section: Angus Dawson

Publisher: Patrick Dawson
Managing Editor: Felicity Laughton
Administration: Elizabeth Taylor
Advertising sales and marketing:
John Sadler, Kirsty Holmes

Photography credits

Front cover: Traditional matador costume
Copyright: anakondasp/shutterstock
Back cover top: Botanical Gardens,
Málaga
Copyright: evantravels/shutterstock
Back cover bottom: El Torcal de
Antequera
Copyright: Arturbudzowski/
Dreamstime.com

Colour section
Inside front cover: shutterstock: Marques,
klublu; superstock: Rafael Jáuregui/age
fotostock. **Page 1**: superstock: Chris Warren/
Chris Warren. **Page 2**: superstock: Mario
Moreno/age fotostock. **Page 4**: superstock:
Jerónimo Alba/age fotostock, Carlos S.
Pereyra/age fotostock; shutterstock: klublu/
Shutterstock.com. **Page 5**: shutterstock:
Algefoto, David Herraez Calzada, Anilah;
superstock: Lucas Vallecillos/age fotostock.
Page 7: superstock: Eduardo Grund/age
fotostock, Robert Harding Picture Library/
Robert Harding Picture Library. **Page 8**:
superstock: Jörgen Larsson/age fotostock.

Printed in Spain by GraphyCems

The content of *Málaga 3rd edition* has
been taken directly from Footprint's
Andalucía Handbook 8th edition.

Publishing information

Footprint Málaga
3rd edition
© Footprint Handbooks Ltd
April 2015

ISBN: 978 1 910120 42 2
CIP DATA: A catalogue record for this
book is available from the British Library

® Footprint Handbooks and the
Footprint mark are a registered
trademark of Footprint Handbooks Ltd

Published by Footprint
6 Riverside Court
Lower Bristol Road
Bath BA2 3DZ, UK
T +44 (0)1225 469141
F +44 (0)1225 469461
footprinttravelguides.com

Distributed in the USA by
National Book Network, Inc.

Every effort has been made to ensure
that the facts in this guidebook are
accurate. However, travellers should still
obtain advice from consulates, airlines,
etc about travel and visa requirements
before travelling. The authors and
publishers cannot accept responsibility
for any loss, injury or inconvenience
however caused.